D1624220

*To*

_____

*From*

_____

*On this date*

_____

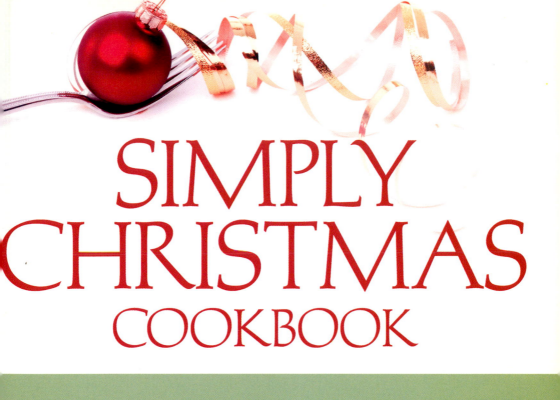

# SIMPLY CHRISTMAS COOKBOOK

• *Recipes for the Holiday Season* •

BARBOUR
PUBLISHING

© 2009 by Barbour Publishing, Inc.

Compiled by Marla Tipton.

ISBN 978-1-60260-578-7

All rights reserved. No part of this publication may be reproduced or transmitted for commercial purposes, except for brief quotations in printed reviews, without written permission of the publisher.

Churches and other noncommercial interests may reproduce portions of this book without the express written permission of Barbour Publishing, provided that the text does not exceed 500 words or that the text is not material quoted from another publisher. When reproducing text from this book, include the following credit line: "From *Simply Christmas Cookbook*, published by Barbour Publishing, Inc. Used by permission."

Published by Barbour Publishing, Inc., P.O. Box 719, Uhrichsville, Ohio 44683, www.barbourbooks.com

*Our mission is to publish and distribute inspirational products offering exceptional value and biblical encouragement to the masses.*

 Member of the
Evangelical Christian
Publishers Association

Printed in the United States of America.

# CONTENTS

If you love celebrating Christmas with a big get-together of family and friends, then this holiday cookbook is just for you. Featuring everything from the best beverages to mouthwatering main dishes and decadent desserts—if it'll top off your seasonal celebration, it's in here. Enjoy!

# Appetizers

*Christmas may be a day of feasting,*
*or of prayer, but always it will be a day*
*of remembrance——a day in which we*
*think of everything we have ever loved.*

Augusta E. Rundel

# COCKTAIL MEATBALLS

1 pound ground beef
½ cup dry bread crumbs
⅓ cup minced onion
¼ cup milk
1 egg
1 tablespoon snipped parsley

1 teaspoon salt
⅛ teaspoon pepper
½ teaspoon Worcestershire sauce
¼ cup shortening
1 (12 ounce) bottle chili sauce
1 (10 ounce) jar grape jelly

In a large bowl, mix ground beef, bread crumbs, onion, milk, egg, parsley, salt, pepper, and Worcestershire sauce. Gently shape into 2-inch balls. In a large skillet, melt shortening. Add meatballs and cook until brown. Remove from skillet and drain. Heat chili sauce and jelly in skillet, stirring constantly until jelly is melted. Add meatballs and stir until thoroughly coated. Simmer uncovered for 30 minutes.

# HOT HAM 'N' SWISS DIP

1 (8 ounce) package cream cheese, softened
⅔ cup mayonnaise
1 tablespoon spicy brown mustard
1½ cups diced fully cooked ham
1 cup grated Swiss cheese
¾ cup cracker crumbs
2 tablespoons butter or margarine, melted

Preheat oven to 400 degrees. Beat cream cheese and mayonnaise until smooth. Add mustard and blend well. Stir in ham and cheese. Spread into pie plate. In small bowl, mix together cracker crumbs and butter and sprinkle over dip mixture. Bake for 12 to 15 minutes.

# BACON-WRAPPED HOT DOGS

2 to 3 packages hot dogs
2 pounds bacon
Toothpicks
2 pounds brown sugar, packed

Slice hot dogs into thirds. Cut bacon slices into thirds. Wrap each hot dog with a cut piece of bacon and hold in place with a toothpick. Place wrapped hot dogs in a slow-cooker until it is full. Pour brown sugar over the hot dogs. Cook on low for 3 to 4 hours.

# SAUSAGE BALLS

½ pound ground pork sausage
½ pound ground spicy pork sausage
2 ounces processed cheese sauce
2 cups buttermilk biscuit mix

Preheat oven to 325 degrees. In a medium bowl, combine regular sausage, spicy sausage, cheese sauce, and biscuit mix. Mix well and form into 1-inch balls. Place on a cookie sheet. Bake 15 to 20 minutes.

# PECAN-STUFFED MUSHROOMS

20 medium-sized mushrooms
3 tablespoons butter, melted
3 ounces cream cheese, softened
2 tablespoons bacon, cooked
    and crumbled
1½ tablespoons chopped pecans
2 tablespoons Italian-style bread crumbs
2 teaspoons minced chives

Gently separate stems from mushroom caps. Brush mushroom caps with the melted butter. Fill each cap with a mixture of cream cheese, bacon, pecans, bread crumbs, and chives. Broil stuffed mushrooms for 3 to 5 minutes. Serve hot.

# CHRISTMAS CHEESE BALL

1 (8 ounce) package cream cheese, softened
4 ounces blue cheese
1 tablespoon green pepper, chopped
1 tablespoon diced pimiento
Chopped walnuts
Minced parsley

In a medium bowl, combine cream cheese, blue cheese, green pepper, and pimiento. Roll into a ball. Roll the ball in the chopped walnuts. Garnish with parsley and serve with crackers.

# PEPPERONI CHEESE BALL

4 (3 ounce) packages cream cheese, softened
¼ cup mayonnaise
⅛ teaspoon garlic powder
⅓ cup Parmesan cheese
½ teaspoon oregano
1 (8 ounce) package pepperoni, chopped

In a large bowl, combine cream cheese, mayonnaise, garlic powder, Parmesan cheese, oregano, and pepperoni; mix well. Form mixture into a ball. Chill in the refrigerator for at least 24 hours. Serve cold with crackers.

# HOLIDAY BEAN DIP

2 (11 ounce) cans white corn, drained
2 (15 ounce) cans black beans, rinsed and drained
½ cup Italian salad dressing
1 cup ranch salad dressing
1 small onion, chopped
1 teaspoon hot pepper sauce
2 teaspoons fresh cilantro, chopped
1 teaspoon chili powder
½ teaspoon ground black pepper

In a medium bowl, thoroughly mix white corn, black beans, Italian salad dressing, ranch salad dressing, onion, hot pepper sauce, cilantro, chili powder, and ground black pepper. Chill in the refrigerator overnight before serving. Serve cold with tortilla chips or crackers.

# CRAB DIP

2 cans crabmeat, drained
1 jar cocktail sauce
2 (8 ounce) packages cream cheese, softened
Lemon slices
Choice of crackers

In a bowl, mix crabmeat and cocktail sauce; set aside. Spread softened cream cheese over a large plate. Pour crab mixture over the cream cheese and garnish with sliced lemons. Serve with crackers.

# HOLIDAY HAM BALLS

3 cups buttermilk baking mix
10½ cups smoked ham, finely chopped
4 cups sharp cheddar cheese, shredded
½ cup Parmesan cheese
2 teaspoons parsley flakes
2 teaspoons spicy brown mustard
⅔ teaspoon milk

Lightly grease a 15½ x 10½-inch jellyroll pan. Mix all ingredients well. Shape mixture into 1-inch balls. Place about 2 inches apart in pan. Bake at 350 degrees for 20 to 25 minutes or until brown. Remove from pan and serve warm.

# CHRISTMAS CHEESE SCONES

2 cups flour
2 teaspoons baking powder
½ teaspoon salt
Pinch cayenne pepper
¼ cup butter
Milk (to create a fairly firm dough)
3 ounces cheese, shredded

Mix flour, baking powder, salt, and pepper. Cut in the butter; mix in just enough milk to incorporate. On a floured surface, roll dough to ½-inch thick. Cut into rounds and place on greased cookie sheet. Brush tops with milk and sprinkle with grated cheese. Cook at 400 degrees for 10 minutes. Cool on a wire rack.

# Corn Chip Dip

1 large can refried beans
1 package taco seasoning mix
1 (8 ounce) container sour cream
1 can black olives, chopped
2 cups cheddar cheese, shredded

In a small bowl, combine beans and taco mix. Spread over the bottom of a microwave-safe dish. Cover with sour cream. Sprinkle olives and cheese over top. Microwave on high (100%) until cheese is melted. Serve hot with corn chips.

# Avocado Dip

2 ripe avocados
½ cup mayonnaise
¾ cup cheddar cheese, shredded
1 cup sour cream
2 tablespoons lemon juice

In a medium bowl, combine all of the ingredients. Beat with an electric hand mixer, on low speed, for 2 minutes. Cover and refrigerate before serving. Serve with tortilla chips or party crackers.

# SIMPLE CRAB DIP

1 (8 ounce) package cream cheese, softened
1 onion, diced
1 can crabmeat, drained
Cocktail sauce

In a medium bowl, combine cream cheese, onion, and crabmeat; mix well. Spoon the mixture onto the center of a serving tray, and spread with cocktail sauce over top. Surround the dip with crackers.

# CHRISTMAS SHRIMP DIP

1 (10 ounce) can tomato soup
½ (8 ounce) package cream cheese, softened
1 envelope gelatin
½ cup water
1 cup mayonnaise
½ cup onion, chopped
½ cup celery, chopped
Baby shrimp

In a small saucepan, cook undiluted soup; melt cream cheese in it. In a separate saucepan, dissolve gelatin in water. Add mayonnaise, onion, and celery to the soup mixture. Stir in the gelatin mixture and refrigerate overnight. Serve cold with baby shrimp.

# CARAMEL CORN

1 cup butter
2 cups brown sugar
1 cup dark Karo syrup
1 teaspoon salt
1 teaspoon vanilla
½ teaspoon baking soda
6 quarts popped corn

In medium saucepan, melt butter; stir in brown sugar, Karo syrup, and salt. Boil 5 minutes. Do not stir. Remove from heat. Stir in vanilla and baking soda. Pour over popped corn and stir. Be sure all corn gets coated. Bake at 250 degrees for 1 hour in a lightly greased baking pan. Stir every 15 minutes.

# CHICKEN BITES

4 boneless, skinless chicken breasts
1 cup finely crushed round butter crackers (about 24)
½ cup Parmesan cheese, grated
¼ cup walnuts, finely chopped
1 teaspoon dried thyme leaves
1 teaspoon dried basil leaves
½ teaspoon seasoned salt
¼ teaspoon black pepper
½ cup butter or margarine, melted

Place aluminum foil over 2 baking sheets. Cut chicken into 1-inch pieces. Combine cracker crumbs, Parmesan cheese, walnuts, thyme, basil, seasoned salt, and pepper. Heat oven to 400 degrees. Dip chicken pieces into melted butter, then into crumb mixture. Place chicken pieces on cookie sheets and bake, uncovered, for 20 to 25 minutes or until golden brown. Makes about 6 dozen appetizers.

# CRAB-STUFFED MUSHROOMS

1 (6 ounce) tin crabmeat

1 egg, well beaten

¼ cup fine bread crumbs

¼ cup tomato juice

1 teaspoon lemon juice

1 dash Tabasco

1 teaspoon onion, finely chopped

2 teaspoons celery, finely chopped

½ teaspoon salt

1 pound mushrooms

½ cup fine bread crumbs

¼ cup butter or margarine, melted

Combine the first nine ingredients and fill mushroom caps with the mixture. Toss remaining bread crumbs with melted butter and sprinkle over filled caps. Brown 6 inches from heat for 5 to 8 minutes, or bake at 350 degrees for 15 to 20 minutes.

# SPICY NACHO CHEESE DIP

1 (1 pound) hot sausage roll
1 (10 ounce) can nacho cheese soup
2 (10 ounce) cans cheddar cheese soup
Jalapeños to taste, chopped

Preheat oven to 350 degrees. In a large skillet, brown and crumble sausage over medium heat; drain. In a casserole dish, combine cooked sausage, undiluted nacho and cheddar soups, and jalapeños; stir. Bake for 20 to 25 minutes. Serve with tortilla chips.

# PUMPKIN DIP

1 (8 ounce) package cream cheese, softened
2 cups powdered sugar
1 (15 ounce) can solid-pack pumpkin
1 tablespoon cinnamon
1 tablespoon pumpkin pie spice
1 teaspoon frozen orange juice concentrate

In a medium bowl, combine cream cheese and sugar; mix until smooth. Stir in the pumpkin. Add the cinnamon, pumpkin pie spice, and orange juice. Mix until well blended. Chill in the refrigerator 1 hour before serving. Hollow a miniature pumpkin and place dip inside just before serving. Serve with apple wedges and gingersnaps.

# CHICKEN CHEESE BALL

2 (8 ounce) packages cream cheese, softened
1 (1 ounce) package ranch dressing mix
1 (5 ounce) can chunk white chicken, drained
½ cup pecans, chopped

In a medium bowl, combine cream cheese, ranch dressing mix, and chicken. Form the mixture into a ball. On a piece of waxed paper, spread out the chopped pecans. Roll the ball in the pecans until it is completely coated. Wrap in plastic and refrigerate for at least 1 hour.

# EASY TACO DIP

1 (8 ounce) package cream cheese, softened
1 cup sour cream
1 package taco seasoning, or to taste
1 cup iceberg lettuce, chopped
1 cup tomatoes, chopped and drained
Green onions, chopped
Cheddar cheese, shredded

Combine first three ingredients and spread in shallow round dish. Layer with iceberg lettuce and tomatoes. Top with green onions and cheese. Serve with tortilla chips.

# GUACAMOLE BITES

2 tubes refrigerated crescent rolls
½ teaspoon cumin
½ teaspoon chili powder
1 (8 ounce) package cream cheese, softened
1½ cups guacamole or 3 mashed ripe avocados
1 tomato, chopped
¼ cup bacon bits
¼ cup sliced ripe black olives

Preheat oven to 375 degrees. Separate crescent rolls into long rectangles, place on ungreased cookie sheet, and press over bottom of sheet. Sprinkle with cumin and chili powder. Bake 17 minutes or until golden brown. Cool. Combine cream cheese and guacamole until smooth, spread over crust, and chill. Top with remaining ingredients. Makes 60 appetizers.

# NUTS AND BOLTS

4 to 5 tablespoons butter or margarine
2 teaspoons Worcestershire sauce
1½ teaspoons onion powder
1½ teaspoons garlic or seasoned salt
2 cups toasted oats cereal
2 cups corn squares cereal
2 cups wheat squares cereal
2 cups pretzels

Melt butter or margarine. Add Worcestershire sauce and spices. Combine all other ingredients in large microwave-safe dish. Add melted mixture and stir well. Microwave on high for 4 to 5 minutes, stirring twice. Cool.

# SHRIMP SPREAD

2 (8 ounce) packages cream cheese, softened
½ cup mayonnaise
½ cup lemon juice
2 (4.5 ounce) cans cocktail shrimp, rinsed, drained, and chopped
1 tablespoon prepared horseradish
1 to 2 tablespoons green onion, finely chopped
⅛ teaspoon garlic salt

In mixing bowl, beat cream cheese until fluffy. Beat in mayonnaise and lemon juice. Stir in shrimp, then add remaining ingredients. Refrigerate to blend flavors, then serve with crackers or vegetables.

# BEVERAGES

---

*Good news from heaven the angels bring,*
*Glad tidings to the earth they sing:*
*To us this day a child is given,*
*To crown us with the joy of heaven.*

MARTIN LUTHER

# COFFEE SLUSH

3 cups strong coffee, hot
2 cups sugar
1 pint half-and-half

1 quart milk
2 teaspoons vanilla

Dissolve sugar in hot coffee. Cool completely. Add remaining ingredients and blend well. Freeze mixture. Thaw for 2 hours before serving.

# HOT APPLE CIDER

2 quarts apple cider
8 whole cloves

8 whole allspice
1 stick cinnamon

In large saucepan, combine ingredients; bring to a boil. Reduce heat and simmer, uncovered, for 10 to 20 minutes. Remove spices before serving.

# HOT CRANBERRY CIDER

1 quart apple cider
1 (32 ounce) bottle cranberry juice
½ cup lemon juice
½ cup firmly packed light brown sugar
8 whole cloves
2 cinnamon sticks

In large saucepan, combine ingredients; bring to a boil. Reduce heat and simmer, uncovered, for 10 minutes. Remove spices before serving.

# CHRISTMAS PUNCH

1 quart grape juice
1 pint lemon juice
1 liter carbonated water
1 pint ginger ale or sweet juice
1 pint orange juice
½ pint pineapple juice

Mix all ingredients and pour into punch bowl with block of ice. Pineapple or orange slices may be used as garnish. Makes about 2 gallons of punch.

# EGGNOG

4 eggs, separated
½ cup sugar, divided
2 cups cold milk
1 cup cold light cream

1½ teaspoons vanilla
⅛ teaspoon salt
¼ teaspoon nutmeg

Beat egg yolks together with ¼ cup sugar until thick. Gradually mix in milk, cream, vanilla, salt, and nutmeg, beating until frothy. Beat egg whites with remaining sugar until mixture forms soft peaks; fold into egg yolk mixture. Cover and chill. Mix well before serving and sprinkle with nutmeg.

# FRUIT SLUSH

1 medium can frozen orange juice concentrate, thawed
½ cup lemon juice
2 cans crushed pineapple, with juice
3 cups water
2 cups sugar
3 to 4 diced bananas
1 (10 ounce) jar maraschino cherries

Mix all ingredients together and put in freezer until slushy, or freeze and take out to thaw until slushy.

# WASSAIL

2 quarts apple juice
2 cups orange juice
1 cup lemon juice
1 (18 ounce) can pineapple juice
1 stick cinnamon
1 teaspoon ground cloves
½ cup sugar

In large saucepan, combine all ingredients; bring to a boil. Reduce heat and simmer, uncovered, for 1 hour. Serve warm.

# EGGNOG PUNCH

1 quart sherbet, any flavor,
   softened
2 cups orange juice

2 cups pineapple juice
1 quart eggnog
Additional sherbet

In large mixing bowl, beat sherbet until smooth. Mix in orange and pineapple juices. Gradually pour in eggnog and blend thoroughly. Pour mixture into a punch bowl and scoop additional sherbet to float on top.

# CREAMY DREAMY HOT CHOCOLATE

1 (14 ounce) can sweetened condensed milk
½ cup unsweetened cocoa powder
2 teaspoons vanilla
⅛ teaspoon salt
6½ cups hot water

In large saucepan, combine first four ingredients; mix well. Over medium heat, slowly stir in water. Cook until heated through, stirring frequently.

# ORANGE SPICED TEA

1 cup powdered orange drink mix
1 heaping cup lemon instant tea, unsweetened
3 cups sugar or sugar substitute
1 teaspoon cinnamon
½ teaspoon nutmeg or ground cloves

Mix all ingredients together. Put 3 heaping teaspoons of mix to one medium mug of boiling water. Use more or less to suit your taste.

# DONNA'S CHRISTMAS PUNCH

1 (12 ounce) can frozen concentrated grape juice, thawed and
   undiluted
½ (12 ounce) can frozen cranberry cocktail juice concentrate,
   thawed and undiluted
2 cups orange juice
1 (2 liter) bottle lemon-lime soda
Orange or lime slices

Mix all ingredients together in punch bowl and garnish with orange or
lime slices. Add an ice ring or crushed ice. Depending upon the num-
ber of people at your holiday celebration, you may want to double the
recipe.

# CHRISTMAS PUNCH

3 teaspoons whole cloves
3 teaspoons ground allspice
1 whole nutmeg
Crushed cinnamon sticks (about 3 inches each)
½ cup brown sugar, firmly packed
4 cups orange juice
6 cups cranberry juice
1 cup water
6 ounces frozen lemonade concentrate, thawed and undiluted

Place spices in a spice bag. Put the bag in a saucepan and add the other ingredients. Bring to a boil, stirring often. Cover and reduce heat, letting the mixture simmer for 30 minutes.

# APPLE PIE MILK SHAKE

½ cup milk
½ cup apple pie filling or a slice of apple pie
1 cup vanilla ice cream
½ teaspoon ground cinnamon

Place all ingredients in a blender. Make sure lid is on tight and blend until smooth. Pour into glasses. Can use other flavors of ice cream and pie if desired.

# HOT CHOCOLATE

½ cup sugar
¼ cup unsweetened
  cocoa powder
⅓ cup hot water
4 cups milk
¾ teaspoon vanilla

Cinnamon stick or
  peppermint stick
Whipped topping (optional)
Caramel topping (optional)
Sprinkles (optional)
Maraschino cherries (optional)

In a medium saucepan, mix sugar and cocoa. Stir in water. Stirring constantly, cook over medium heat until mixture boils. After boiling for 2 minutes, add milk. Reduce heat and cook until hot, but do not boil. Remove from heat and add vanilla. Beat with whisk until foamy. Pour into mugs and add a cinnamon or peppermint stick. Top with whipped topping, caramel, sprinkles, and a cherry, if desired. Serves 4 to 6.

# SNOWY CINNAMON COCOA

4 cups milk
1 cup chocolate syrup
1 teaspoon cinnamon
Whipped topping
¼ cup semi-sweet chocolate chips

Place milk and chocolate syrup in a microwave-safe bowl and stir. Cook on high for 3 to 4 minutes or until hot. Stir in cinnamon. Pour into 4 large mugs and garnish with whipped topping and chocolate chips.

# TROPICAL FRUIT PUNCH

1 cup sugar
1 cup water
3 cups grapefruit juice
3 cups orange juice

3 cups pineapple juice
½ cup lemon juice
½ cup lime juice
1 (2 liter) bottle ginger ale, chilled

In a saucepan, combine sugar and water; bring to a boil. Boil for 2 minutes, stirring constantly. Remove from heat and allow to cool. Pour into a punch bowl and add juices. Cover and refrigerate until ready to serve. Add ginger ale immediately before serving.

# ANGEL FROST PUNCH

2 (10 ounce) packages frozen sliced strawberries
2 (6 ounce) cans frozen pink lemonade concentrate, undiluted
2 cups water
1 quart vanilla ice cream
2 cups lemon-lime soda, chilled

Combine 1 package strawberries, 1 can lemonade concentrate, 1 cup water, and half of the ice cream in blender. Blend until thick and smooth. Pour into a punch bowl. Repeat the process with remaining strawberries, lemonade concentrate, water, and ice cream. Carefully pour soda down the side of the punch bowl. Gently stir to mix.

# CHERRY SPARKLE PUNCH

1½ ounces cherry-flavored powdered drink mix
1 cup sugar
2 cups milk
1 quart vanilla ice cream
1 quart lemon-lime soda

Combine first two ingredients; dissolve with milk. Add ice cream in small scoops. Slowly add soda. Stir slightly.

# HOT CAPPUCCINO

1 cup instant hot chocolate mix
½ cup high-quality instant coffee granules
½ cup powdered nondairy coffee creamer
½ cup powdered skim milk
1¼ teaspoons ground cinnamon
¼ teaspoon ground nutmeg
Boiling water
Chocolate, grated (optional)

Mix dry ingredients well. Use ¼ cup mixture for each 2 cups boiling water. Blend desired amount until foamy and pour into mugs. Sprinkle with grated chocolate, if desired.

# CANDY CANE COCOA

4 cups milk

3 (1 ounce) squares semisweet chocolate,
    chopped

4 peppermint candy canes, crushed

1 cup whipped cream

4 small peppermint candy canes

In a medium saucepan, heat milk until hot,
but not boiling. Whisk in the chocolate
and the crushed candy canes until smooth.
Pour hot cocoa into 4 mugs. Serve each
with a miniature candy cane stirring stick.

# HOT FRUIT PUNCH

1 (6 ounce) can frozen orange juice concentrate, undiluted
10 cups water
1 teaspoon vanilla
1 (6 ounce) can frozen lemonade concentrate, undiluted
1½ cups sugar
1 teaspoon almond extract

In a large saucepan, combine all ingredients. Heat slowly, but do not bring to a boil.

# PERKY PUNCH

1 small can orange juice concentrate, thawed
1 small can lemonade concentrate, thawed
1 envelope strawberry Kool-Aid (unsweetened)
1 envelope cherry Kool-Aid (unsweetened)
1 tall can tropical fruit punch
2 (12 ounce) bottles ginger ale

Prepare orange juice and lemonade according to directions on cans. Add Kool-Aid, using half the amount of water and sugar required. Add tropical fruit punch. Pour into punch bowl; add ginger ale and ice cubes.

# MALTED MILK BALL CHILLER

⅓ cup malted milk balls, crushed
1 cup ice cream
1½ tablespoons chocolate syrup
½ cup milk

Place ingredients into blender and mix until creamy. Pour into a glass. Serve immediately.

# MINT COCOA

15 chocolate sandwich cookies, crushed
3 cups milk
⅓ cup chocolate syrup
¼ teaspoon peppermint extract
4 tablespoons whipped topping
4 pinches cinnamon

Place sandwich cookies, milk, chocolate syrup, and peppermint extract in a blender and cover. Blend on high speed until well mixed. Pour into a medium saucepan and cook over medium heat until heated through. Pour into 4 mugs. Top each mug with 1 tablespoon whipped topping and a pinch of cinnamon.

# BREADS

*Christmas Eve was a night of song that wrapped itself about you like a shawl. But it warmed more than your body. It warmed your heart. . .filled it, too, with melody that would last forever.*

BESS STREETER ALDRICH

# REFRIGERATOR ROLLS

2 cups boiling water
1½ cups sugar
1 tablespoon salt
½ cup shortening
2 scant tablespoons active
    dry yeast (2 packages)

1 cup lukewarm water
1 teaspoon sugar
2 eggs, beaten
10 to 11 cups flour
    (sapphire is best)

Pour boiling water over 1½ cups sugar. Add salt and shortening. Let cool until lukewarm. Dissolve yeast in lukewarm water. Add 1 teaspoon sugar and the eggs. Mix well and add to first mixture. Beat in flour until dough pulls away from the sides of the bowl. Cover dough with cloth and let rise until double in size. Punch down dough. Form rolls (about golf ball-sized). Place in greased pan and let rise until doubled. Bake at 375 degrees for about 12 minutes.

NOTE: *Keep hands greased while forming rolls. For 12 rolls use a 13 x 9 x 2-inch pan. For 8 rolls use a round cake pan. Unused dough may be stored in refrigerator until ready to use.*

# GRANDMA'S BISCUIT MIX

2 cups flour
4 teaspoons baking powder
½ teaspoon plus 2 dashes salt
½ teaspoon cream of tartar

Sift above ingredients and place in a 1-pint jar. Attach a recipe card with the following instructions:

# GRANDMA'S BISCUITS

Grandma's Biscuit Mix
½ cup butter
⅔ cup milk
1 tablespoon mayonnaise

Preheat oven to 450 degrees. Place Grandma's Biscuit Mix in a bowl; cut in butter then make a well in the center of the ingredients. Combine milk and mayonnaise with mixture, and gently mix until all ingredients are combined. On floured surface, roll dough ½-inch thick. Cut with 2-inch biscuit cutter and place close together on an ungreased cookie sheet. Bake for 12 to 15 minutes. Serve warm with butter and honey—Yum!

GIFT IDEAS: *Attach biscuit cutter with a ribbon to the jar mix, or give gift in a basket with biscuit mix, biscuit cutter, and honey or jam.*

# BACON-ONION PAN ROLLS

1 pound frozen bread dough, thawed
¼ cup butter, melted and divided
½ pound sliced bacon, cooked and crumbled
½ cup chopped onion

On a lightly floured board, roll dough to ¼-inch thickness. Cut rolls using a 2½-inch biscuit cutter. Brush rolls using 3 tablespoons melted butter. Place 1 teaspoon each of bacon and onion on half of each roll. Fold over and pinch to seal. With pinched sides up, place rolls in a greased 9-inch square baking pan, forming 3 rows of 6. Brush tops with remaining butter. Let rise until doubled, about 30 minutes. Bake at 350 degrees for 25 to 30 minutes or until golden brown.

# BLUEBERRY MUFFIN MIX

1¾ cups all-purpose flour
½ cup sugar
2 teaspoons baking powder
1 teaspoon dried, grated lemon peel

In a medium bowl, combine all ingredients. Spoon muffin mix into a 1-pint glass jar. Attach a recipe card with the following instructions:

# BLUEBERRY MUFFINS

Blueberry Muffin Mix
1 egg, slightly beaten
¾ cup milk
¼ cup oil
¾ cup fresh or frozen blueberries

Preheat oven to 400 degrees. Line muffin tin with paper baking cups. In a large bowl, empty Blueberry Muffin Mix. Add egg, milk, and oil, stirring with a spoon until combined. Fold in blueberries. Pour batter into baking cups until ⅔ full. Bake for 20 minutes or until lightly golden. Remove muffins from tin to a wire rack to cool slightly. Serve warm.

# PECAN SWEET ROLL RINGS

2 (8 ounce) tubes refrigerated crescent rolls
4 tablespoons butter, melted and divided
½ cup chopped pecans
¼ cup sugar
1 teaspoon ground cinnamon
½ teaspoon ground nutmeg
½ cup powdered sugar
2 tablespoons maple syrup

Separate crescent dough into 8 rectangles. Seal the perforations. Brush rectangles using 2 tablespoons butter. Mix the pecans, sugar, cinnamon, and nutmeg. Sprinkle 1 tablespoon of the pecan mixture over each rectangle. Press lightly into the dough. Roll each rectangle up jellyroll style, starting at the long side. Seal the seams. Twist each roll 2 or 3 times. Cut 6 shallow diagonal slits in each roll. Shape each roll into a ring, pinching ends to seal. Place on a greased baking sheet and brush with remaining butter. Bake at 375 degrees for 12 to 14 minutes or until golden brown. Combine powdered sugar and maple syrup until smooth. Drizzle over warm rolls.

# MAPLE-NUT BREAKFAST MUFFIN MIX

1 cup whole wheat flour
1¼ cups all-purpose flour
2 teaspoons baking powder

½ teaspoon baking soda
¼ teaspoon salt
¼ cup finely chopped pecans

In a medium bowl, combine all ingredients. Spoon muffin mix into a 1-pint glass jar, tapping slightly to settle ingredients. Attach a recipe card with the following instructions:

# MAPLE-NUT BREAKFAST MUFFINS

Maple-Nut Breakfast Muffin Mix
3 large eggs, slightly beaten
¼ cup honey
¼ cup maple syrup
⅔ cup oil
1 cup milk
1 teaspoon vanilla

Preheat oven to 375 degrees. Grease a 12-cup muffin tin, or line muffin tin with paper baking cups. In a large bowl, empty Maple-Nut Breakfast Muffin Mix. Make a well in the center and add remaining ingredients. Stir with spoon until just combined. Fill baking cups ⅔ full. Bake for 15 to 17 minutes or until lightly golden. Remove muffins from tin and cool on wire rack.

# PECAN STICKY BUN

½ cup chopped pecans
1 package frozen dinner rolls
½ cup butter

½ cup sugar
½ cup brown sugar
1 teaspoon cinnamon

Grease a Bundt or angel food pan. Sprinkle bottom of pan with chopped pecans and place frozen rolls on top of nuts. In a saucepan, melt butter, sugar, brown sugar, and cinnamon. Pour mixture over rolls. Cover rolls and allow to stand overnight. Bake at 350 degrees for 25 minutes.

# CHOCOLATE CHIP SOUR CREAM BANANA BREAD

½ cup butter
1 (3 ounce) package cream cheese
1 cup sugar
2 eggs
2 teaspoons vanilla
1½ cups flour

1 teaspoon baking soda
½ teaspoon salt
1 cup mashed bananas
½ cup nuts, chopped
1 cup mini chocolate chips
½ cup sour cream

Preheat oven to 350 degrees. Cream butter, cream cheese, and sugar. Mix in eggs and vanilla. Gradually add dry ingredients. Stir in mashed bananas, nuts, chocolate chips, and sour cream. Divide into two greased loaf pans and bake for 1 hour.

# CRANBERRY SCONES

1¾ cups flour
1 tablespoon baking powder
½ teaspoon salt
1 cup quick or old-fashioned oats
½ cup butter
½ cup chopped pecans
½ cup dried cranberries
½ teaspoon dried orange peel
⅓ cup honey
¼ cup milk
1 egg, lightly beaten

Preheat oven to 375 degrees. In a medium bowl, mix together flour, baking powder, salt, and oats. Cut butter into dry ingredients. Mix in pecans, cranberries, and orange peel. In small bowl, whisk together honey, milk, and egg. Pour wet ingredients over dry and stir with fork just until dough begins to hold together. Turn dough out onto floured surface and gently knead 8 to 10 times. Pat dough into circle. Place on greased cookie sheet. Cut dough into wedges and separate them slightly. Bake for 10 to 12 minutes or until light golden brown.

# FESTIVE BUBBLE LOAF

¾ cup butter, divided

½ cup brown sugar

1 small jar maraschino cherries, drained and coarsely chopped

1 cup pecan halves

1 cup sugar

2 teaspoons cinnamon

1 (24 count) package frozen dinner rolls

In a microwave-safe bowl, melt ¼ cup butter. Stir in brown sugar. Pour into bottom of well-greased tube pan. Place cherries and pecans over sugar. Melt ½ cup butter; stir in sugar and cinnamon. Roll each frozen roll in cinnamon-sugar mixture. Arrange in tube pan. Cover and let rise overnight. Bake at 350 degrees for 30 minutes. Cool 10 minutes, then invert onto serving plate.

# HOLIDAY BUNS

4 cups warm water

1 cup sugar

1 package active dry yeast

1 egg

3 teaspoons salt

1 cup oil

10 cups flour

1 cup raisins (optional)

2 teaspoons cinnamon
(optional)

Combine water, sugar, and yeast. Cover and let stand 10 minutes. Mix in egg, salt, oil, and flour, and let rise until doubled. Put into cupcake tins for round rolls. Bake at 350 degrees for 20 minutes.

VARIATION: *For raisin bread, add raisins and cinnamon after dough has risen.*

# Oatmeal Dinner Rolls

1 cup quick or old-fashioned oats
3 tablespoons butter
2 cups boiling water

Place oats and butter in large mixing bowl. Pour in boiling water and let mixture stand for 20 minutes.

2 packages dry yeast
⅓ cup warm water

In small bowl, dissolve yeast in warm water.

In another bowl, mix together:
¾ cup brown sugar
1 tablespoon sugar
1½ teaspoons salt
4 cups all-purpose flour
1 to 1½ cups whole wheat flour

Stir yeast into oatmeal mixture, then gradually mix in dry ingredients. Add enough flour to form a soft dough. Cover and let rise until doubled; form into dinner rolls and place in greased baking pans. Let rise again until double. Bake at 350 degrees for 20 to 30 minutes.

# HONEY WHOLE WHEAT BREAD

3 cups boiling water

1½ cups old-fashioned oats

¾ cup honey

6 tablespoons oil

3 packages dry yeast

½ cup warm water

5 cups whole wheat flour

2½ cups unbleached white flour

3 teaspoons salt

Pour 3 cups boiling water into large mixing bowl. Stir in oats; allow mixture to cool to lukewarm. Add honey and oil. Dissolve yeast in ½ cup warm water, then add to oatmeal mixture. In another mixing bowl, combine flours and salt. Stir 6 cups of flour mixture into oatmeal mixture. Gradually knead in additional flour to make a soft dough. Knead an additional 5 to 10 minutes. Let rise in covered bowl until double. Punch down dough, then knead again for 5 to 10 minutes. Form into loaves and place in greased loaf pans. Let rise 30 minutes. Bake at 325 degrees for 1 hour. Cool on wire racks.

# PUMPKIN SPICE BREAD MIX

1 cup sugar
1 cup brown sugar, packed
3½ cups all-purpose flour
2 teaspoons baking soda
½ teaspoon baking powder
1 teaspoon salt
1 tablespoon pumpkin pie spice
1 cup chopped pecans

In a 1-quart wide-mouthed jar, layer ingredients in order given, combining flour, baking soda, baking powder, salt, and spice. Attach a recipe card with the following instructions:

# PUMPKIN SPICE BREAD

¾ cup oil
4 eggs
1 (15 ounce) can pumpkin
2 teaspoons vanilla
Pumpkin Spice Bread Mix
⅔ cup water

Preheat oven to 325 degrees. Grease and flour two 9 x 5 x 3-inch loaf pans. In a large mixing bowl, combine oil, eggs, pumpkin, and vanilla. Add Pumpkin Spice Bread Mix alternately with water. Spoon batter into prepared pans. Bake for 1 hour and 15 minutes or until toothpick inserted near center comes out clean. Let cool in pans for 10 minutes before turning out onto a wire rack.

# NEVER-FAIL CRESCENTS

1 cup milk, lukewarm
½ cup oil
½ cup sugar
1 teaspoon salt

2 packages dry yeast
3 eggs, beaten
4½ to 5½ cups flour

Mix first six ingredients; let mixture sit for 15 to 20 minutes. Gradually add enough flour so that dough pulls away from sides of bowl. Cover and let rise until dough doubles in size. Divide dough into three sections. On a floured surface, roll out dough into circle and cut into 8 triangles. Roll each triangle into a crescent shape and place on greased baking sheet. Let crescents rise, approximately 1 hour. Bake at 375 degrees for 10 minutes or until light golden brown.

# BUTTERMILK YEAST BUNS

¼ cup warm water (100 degrees–115 degrees)
1 package active dry yeast
3 cups buttermilk, room temperature
½ cup sugar
½ cup butter, melted
2 eggs, beaten
1 teaspoon baking soda
1 teaspoon salt
8 cups all-purpose flour
Additional butter, melted

Pour water into a large mixing bowl. Crumble yeast into water, stirring to dissolve. Add buttermilk and sugar; allow to stand for 15 minutes. Add warm butter and beaten eggs; mix. Sift baking soda and salt with half of the flour. Add soda mixture to liquid mixture. Beat until a smooth batter forms. Add remaining flour. Stir with spoon until dough is no longer sticky. Knead on a floured surface. Place in a large greased bowl. Turn once to be sure the top is greased. Cover and let rise until doubled (about 1 hour). Punch dough down and form into buns by squeezing dough into egg-sized balls. Place on a greased baking sheet and flatten slightly. Let rise until doubled (about 30 minutes). Bake at 400 degrees for 15 to 20 minutes or until light golden brown. Remove to cooling rack and brush top with melted butter.

# DINNER ROLLS

1 cup butter
1 cup sugar
1 cup milk
2 packages dry yeast
1 cup warm water

1 teaspoon sugar
2 teaspoons salt
2 eggs, lightly beaten
6 cups flour
Melted butter

Over low heat, melt 1 cup butter with 1 cup sugar and milk. Remove from heat and cool to lukewarm. In large mixing bowl, dissolve yeast in warm water with 1 teaspoon sugar. Mix in butter mixture, then salt and eggs. Blend thoroughly. Gradually stir in flour. Place in greased bowl; cover and let rise until doubled. Punch down; form into rolls, then place on greased baking sheets and let rise again. Brush tops with melted butter and bake at 350 degrees 9 to 12 minutes or until golden.

# CINNAMON STICKY BUNS

1 cup brown sugar, packed
½ cup corn syrup
½ cup butter
1 cup pecans, coarsely chopped

½ cup sugar
¼ cup ground cinnamon
2 (17.3 ounce) tubes large
   refrigerated biscuits

In a saucepan, mix brown sugar, corn syrup, and butter. Cook until sugar dissolves, stirring constantly. Add pecans to mixture. Spoon into a greased 13 x 9 x 2-inch baking pan. In a shallow bowl, mix sugar and cinnamon. Cut each biscuit in half and dip in cinnamon mixture. Bake at 375 degrees for 25 to 30 minutes or until golden.

# DINNER ROLLS

4¼ to 4¾ cups flour

1 package active dry yeast

1 cup milk

⅓ cup sugar

⅓ cup butter

¾ teaspoon salt

2 eggs, beaten

In large mixing bowl, stir together 2 cups of the flour and the yeast. In medium saucepan, heat and stir milk, sugar, butter, and salt until warm (120 degrees) and butter almost melts. Add milk mixture to dry mix along with eggs; mix well using hands. Mix in the remaining flour. Knead in enough to make moderately stiff dough that is smooth and elastic. Shape into ball. Place in lightly greased bowl. Turn once; cover and let rise until doubled, about 1 hour. Divide dough in half; cover and let rest for 10 minutes. Lightly grease cookie sheets. Shape into desired rolls; cover and let rise in warm place until nearly double, about 30 minutes. Bake at 375 degrees for 12 to 15 minutes or until golden.

# CRANBERRY WALNUT STREUSEL BREAD

1½ cups flour
1 teaspoon baking soda
1 teaspoon baking powder
1 teaspoon cinnamon
½ teaspoon salt
1 cup sugar
2 eggs, lightly beaten
2 tablespoons butter or margarine, melted
2 teaspoons orange zest
½ cup orange juice
1 cup fresh or frozen cranberries
½ cup chopped walnuts
½ cup raisins

Streusel:
¼ cup flour
2 tablespoons sugar
½ teaspoon cinnamon
2 tablespoons butter

Preheat oven to 350 degrees. Grease and flour loaf pan. In small bowl, stir together flour, baking soda, baking powder, cinnamon, and salt. In large mixing bowl, beat together sugar, eggs, butter, and orange zest. Alternating between wet and dry, gradually mix in the dry ingredients and orange juice. Stir in cranberries, nuts, and raisins. Pour into prepared pan. In small bowl, combine flour, sugar, and cinnamon. Cut in butter. Sprinkle over bread batter. Bake for 1 hour 15 minutes or until toothpick inserted in the center comes out clean. Cool for 10 minutes, then remove to wire rack to cool completely.

# Breakfast Dishes

*Christmas is not a time or a season but a state of mind. To cherish peace and goodwill, to be plenteous in mercy, is to have the real spirit of Christmas. If we think on these things, there will be born in us a Savior and over us will shine a star sending its gleam of hope to the world.*

Calvin Coolidge

# BREAKFAST CASSEROLE

1 pound sausage

6 eggs, beaten

1 teaspoon salt

1 teaspoon dry mustard

1 cup cheese, shredded

1 cup milk

2 slices day-old bread, torn

Brown and drain sausage. Combine sausage and remaining ingredients in a two-quart casserole dish. Bake uncovered at 350 degrees for 45 minutes.

# APPLE OVEN PANCAKE

2 tablespoons butter or margarine
2 tablespoons brown sugar
¼ teaspoon cinnamon
1 medium apple, peeled and thinly sliced
2 eggs
½ cup flour
¼ teaspoon salt
½ cup milk
1 teaspoon vanilla

Heat oven to 400 degrees. Melt butter in pie plate in the oven. Remove from oven and brush butter up sides of pie plate. In small dish, mix together brown sugar and cinnamon. Sprinkle brown sugar mixture over butter. Layer apple slices over sugar. In medium bowl, beat eggs. Stir in remaining ingredients just until blended. Bake 30 to 35 minutes, then immediately invert onto serving plate. Serve with syrup, if desired.

# COUNTRY BREAKFAST CASSEROLE

½ pound spicy or mild bulk pork sausage
½ cup onion, finely chopped
4 cups frozen diced hash brown potatoes, thawed
    (about half a 32-ounce package)
1½ cups Colby/Monterey Jack cheese, shredded
3 eggs, beaten
1 cup milk
¼ teaspoon pepper
Salsa

In a large skillet, thoroughly brown sausage and onion. Drain. In an 8 x 8 x 2-inch baking dish, layer potatoes, half of the cheese, sausage mixture, and remaining cheese. Combine eggs, milk, and pepper; pour over cheese. (May be covered and chilled overnight if necessary.) Bake, covered, at 350 degrees for 50 to 55 minutes or until a knife inserted near center comes out clean. Transfer to a wire rack. Let stand for 10 minutes. Cut into squares and serve with salsa.

# BISCUIT COFFEE CAKE

2 cans buttermilk refrigerator biscuits
⅓ cup brown sugar, firmly packed
¼ cup butter, melted
1 teaspoon cinnamon
⅓ cup pecans

Preheat oven to 350 degrees. In a lightly greased 9 x 9-inch pan, arrange biscuits, overlapping edges. Combine remaining ingredients and spread evenly over biscuits. Bake for 15 minutes or until done.

# BAKED FRENCH TOAST

¾ cup brown sugar, packed
1 teaspoon cinnamon
½ cup butter
1 loaf French bread, sliced

6 eggs
1½ cups half-and-half
½ cup toasted pecans,
    chopped

In small bowl, mix together brown sugar and cinnamon. Set aside. Melt butter in 13 x 9 x 2-inch baking pan in the oven. Sprinkle one-third of the sugar mixture over butter. Place bread slices in the pan. Sprinkle remaining sugar mixture over bread. Beat eggs and half-and-half; pour over bread. Refrigerate overnight. In the morning, sprinkle pecans over bread. Bake at 350 degrees for 35 to 45 minutes.

# MINI SAUSAGE PIZZAS

2 (5 ounce) jars sharp American cheese spread
¼ cup butter, softened
⅛ teaspoon cayenne pepper
1 pound bulk pork sausage, browned and well drained
12 English muffins, split

In a small mixing bowl, beat cheese, butter, and cayenne pepper. Add sausage and stir well. Spread on cut side of muffins. Place on a baking sheet and bake at 425 degrees for 8 to 10 minutes or until golden brown.

# CINNAMON BISCUITS

4 cans refrigerator biscuits

1½ cups sugar, divided

2½ teaspoons cinnamon, divided

¾ cup butter

Preheat oven to 350 degrees. Cut each biscuit into quarters. In a shallow bowl combine ½ cup sugar and 1 teaspoon cinnamon. Roll biscuits in cinnamon and sugar mixture, making sure they are evenly coated. Grease a Bundt cake pan and drop biscuit pieces in the pan, keeping them evenly distributed. In a small saucepan, mix 1 cup sugar, butter, and 1½ teaspoons cinnamon. Bring to a boil. Pour over biscuits and bake for 45 minutes or until done. Let cool and flip over on a plate. Pull apart to eat.

# BREAKFAST PIZZA

1 (8.5 ounce) can refrigerated crescent rolls
1 pound pork sausage, cooked, crumbled, and drained
1 cup frozen shredded hash brown potatoes, thawed
¼ cup onion, chopped
1 cup sharp cheddar cheese, shredded
5 eggs, lightly beaten
¼ cup milk
½ teaspoon salt
½ teaspoon pepper
¼ cup grated Parmesan cheese

Preheat oven to 375 degrees. Separate crescent rolls into triangles. Place triangles on ungreased 12-inch pizza pan with points toward the center. Press rolls together, sealing perforations. Create small rim around edge of crust. Sprinkle cooked sausage evenly over crust. Top with potatoes and onion. Sprinkle with cheddar cheese. Whisk together eggs, milk, salt, and pepper in small bowl. Pour egg mixture evenly over pizza. Sprinkle with Parmesan cheese. Bake for 15 to 20 minutes or until eggs are set.

# SOUTHERN CORNMEAL WAFFLES

¾ cup yellow cornmeal
⅛ cup flour
¼ teaspoon salt
¼ teaspoon baking soda
½ teaspoon baking powder

1 teaspoon sugar
1 egg, beaten
1 cup milk
2 teaspoons lemon juice
¼ cup oil

Sift the dry ingredients together. Stir in the remaining ingredients. Cook on a greased waffle iron.

# Cutout Doughnuts

1 cup sugar

3 eggs, beaten

4 cups flour

¼ teaspoon cream of tartar

2 teaspoons baking powder

1 cup milk

1 teaspoon vanilla

Pinch of nutmeg

Powdered sugar

Beat together sugar and eggs until foamy. In a separate bowl, mix flour, cream of tartar, and baking powder. Add half of the flour mixture and ½ cup milk to eggs. Stir well. Pour in remaining flour and milk. Stir well. Add vanilla and nutmeg. Stir well, but do not make dough too stiff. Roll dough out on floured surface with a rolling pin until about ½ inch thick. Cut with a cookie cutter, then fry in hot oil until lightly browned. Sprinkle with powdered sugar.

# German Potato Pancakes

6 medium potatoes, peeled and shredded
1 small onion, peeled and grated
2 eggs, beaten
2 tablespoons flour
¼ teaspoon baking powder
1 teaspoon salt
¼ teaspoon pepper
¼ cup oil

Combine shredded potato and onion. Place in colander and squeeze out as much liquid as possible. Working quickly so potatoes do not discolor, beat together eggs, flour, baking powder, salt, and pepper in large mixing bowl. Stir in potatoes and onion. In large skillet, heat oil over medium heat. Drop heaping tablespoonfuls of the potato mixture into the skillet. Press to flatten. Cook about 3 minutes on each side until browned and cooked through. Drain on paper towels.

# FESTIVE BREAKFAST CASSEROLE

½ pound bacon
½ cup onion, chopped
¼ cup green pepper, chopped
¼ cup red pepper, chopped
12 eggs
1 cup milk
1 (16 ounce) package frozen hash browns, thawed
1 cup Colby-Jack cheese, shredded
1 teaspoon salt
½ teaspoon pepper

Preheat oven to 350 degrees. In skillet, fry bacon until crisp. Remove bacon from pan; crumble and set aside. In the drippings, cook onion and green and red peppers until tender. Remove from heat. In large mixing bowl, beat eggs with milk. Stir in hash browns, cheese, salt, pepper, bacon, onion, and peppers. Pour into greased 13 x 9 x 2-inch baking dish. Bake for 35 to 45 minutes.

# HONEY-TOPPED PECAN BREAKFAST BREAD

½ cup sugar
1 to 2 teaspoons cinnamon
¼ cup chopped pecans
2 (8 ounce) cans refrigerated crescent rolls
2 tablespoons butter, melted

Honey Topping:
¼ cup sifted powdered sugar
2 tablespoons honey
2 tablespoons butter
1 teaspoon vanilla
¼ cup pecan halves

Preheat oven to 325 degrees. Mix sugar, cinnamon, and pecans. Set aside. Unroll crescent-roll dough and separate into 16 triangles. Brush each triangle with melted butter and sprinkle with sugar mixture. Roll up each triangle, starting from the shortest side opposite a point and rolling toward the point. Place 8 rolls, point side down, in a greased 9 x 5 x 3-inch loaf pan. Place remaining rolls on top of first layer. Bake for about 55 minutes or until done. Meanwhile, prepare the honey topping by combining all topping ingredients except pecans in a small saucepan. Heat until smooth and bubbly. Gradually stir in pecan halves. Cool for 15 minutes and drizzle over warm bread. Serve immediately.

# CRUSTLESS CHEESE QUICHE

2 cups small-curd cottage cheese
2 cups Monterey Jack cheese, shredded
2 cups cheddar cheese, shredded
4 eggs, lightly beaten
2 tablespoons butter, melted
2 tablespoons ripe olives, chopped
1 (4 ounce) can green chilies, chopped
½ cup flour
1 teaspoon baking powder
½ teaspoon salt
Chopped tomatoes
Additional chopped ripe olives

Preheat oven to 400 degrees. Mix first 7 ingredients together. In a separate bowl, mix flour, baking powder, and salt. Add flour mixture to cheese mixture and mix well. Pour mixture into a greased 9-inch pie plate. Bake for 15 minutes. Reduce heat to 350 degrees and bake 30 minutes longer or until fork inserted in center comes out clean. Use tomatoes and extra olives as a garnish.

# EGGNOG WAFFLES

2 cups biscuit mix
⅔ cup milk
⅔ cup eggnog

1 egg, beaten
2 tablespoons oil
Chopped pecans, optional

In a medium mixing bowl, whisk together first 5 ingredients. In batches, bake waffles on hot waffle iron 5 to 7 minutes or until lightly golden. If desired, sprinkle with chopped pecans before baking. Serve with your favorite syrup or topping.

# BUTTERMILK SCONES

4 cups flour

2 to 4 tablespoons sugar

1½ tablespoons baking powder

1 teaspoon salt

1 teaspoon baking soda

1 teaspoon butter, chilled

1½ cups buttermilk

Preheat oven to 400 degrees. Combine flour, sugar, baking powder, salt, and soda. Cut in butter until mixture resembles coarse crumbs. Make well in center of ingredients. Pour buttermilk into well, then stir until moistened. Turn dough onto a floured board. Knead gently 10 to 12 times. Form into a ball and flatten into a round. Using a pizza cutter, cut into 8 wedges. Place on ungreased baking sheet. Bake for 15 to 20 minutes or until done. Serve warm.

# FRUIT PIZZA

1 package refrigerated sugar cookie dough
1 (8 ounce) package cream cheese
12 ounces whipped topping
½ cup sugar
½ teaspoon vanilla
Mandarin oranges
Fresh fruit: strawberries, kiwi, pineapple, blueberries, banana

Preheat oven according to directions on cookie dough package. Cut cookies in ½-inch slices and arrange on a pizza pan, pressing together to make crust. Bake for 15 to 20 minutes or until done. Combine cream cheese, whipped topping, sugar, and vanilla in a bowl. Stir until smooth and spread over cooled cookie crust. Arrange fruit in layers on cookie crust. Cut into slices.

# SKILLET HAM AND POTATOES

2 tablespoons butter
1½ cups frozen shredded hash browns
½ pound ham, diced
Shredded cheese

Melt butter in a skillet. Add hash browns and cook over medium heat for about 10 minutes, making sure not to let them stick to the bottom. Leave hash browns in the skillet and add ham. Top with cheese. Reduce heat to low and cover the skillet until cheese melts.

# FOUR-LAYER BREAKFAST DISH

1 pound ground sausage
4 eggs
¼ cup milk
1 can crescent rolls
2 to 3 cups mozzarella cheese, shredded

Preheat oven to 350 degrees. In a frying pan, brown sausage; drain excess fat. Beat eggs and milk together. Put rolls in the bottom of a 13 x 9 x 2-inch buttered casserole dish; layer sausage and egg mixture, and top with cheese. Bake for 30 to 50 minutes, until eggs are no longer runny.

# CANDIES

*Christmas is the season for kindling
the fire of hospitality in the hall,
the genial flame of charity in the heart.*

WASHINGTON IRVING

# CHRISTMAS TURTLE CANDIES

Nonstick cooking spray
4 ounces pecans, halved
24 caramels
1 cup (6 ounces) semisweet chocolate chips
1 teaspoon shortening

Preheat oven to 300 degrees. Cover cookie sheet with aluminum foil, shiny side up. Lightly grease foil with cooking spray. Place three pecan halves in Y shape on foil. Place one caramel candy in center of each Y. Repeat. Bake just until caramel is melted, about 9 to 10 minutes. In a saucepan, heat chocolate chips and shortening over low heat just until chocolate is melted. Spread over candies and refrigerate for 30 minutes. Makes 24 turtle candies.

# Peanut Brittle

2¼ cups salted peanuts
2 cups sugar
½ cup light corn syrup

1 cup water
1 teaspoon butter
¼ teaspoon soda

Butter a cookie sheet thoroughly. Spread salted peanuts over the bottom of the cookie sheet. Set aside. In a saucepan, mix sugar, corn syrup, and water. Cook until medium brown in color, about 25 minutes. Be sure to stir often. Remove from heat. Stir in remaining ingredients. Pour over peanuts immediately. Allow to cool. Break into pieces.

# Almond Chocolate Brittle

2 cups white chocolate chips
1 tablespoon oil
½ cup almonds, chopped

Line an 8 x 8-inch square baking dish with foil. In a saucepan over low heat, melt together white chocolate chips and oil. Stir until melted. Add almonds. Pour into prepared baking dish and refrigerate until firm. Break into pieces. Store in an airtight container.

# CHEERY CHERRY CHRISTMAS FUDGE

1 (8 ounce) can almond paste
1 (14 ounce) can sweetened condensed milk, divided
Red food coloring
1¾ cups semisweet chocolate chips
Red candied-cherry halves
Almonds, sliced

Line an 8 x 8-inch baking pan with aluminum foil, extending foil over edges of pan. Beat almond paste and ¼ cup sweetened condensed milk in small bowl until well mixed. Add food coloring and beat until blended. Refrigerate for about 1 hour or until firm. Spread onto bottom of prepared pan. Place chocolate chips and remaining sweetened condensed milk in medium microwave-safe bowl. Microwave on high for 1 to 1½ minutes or until chocolate is melted and smooth. Spread over top of almond paste layer. Cover and refrigerate until firm. Use edges of foil to lift fudge out of pan. Peel off foil and cut fudge into squares. Garnish with cherry halves and almonds. Store in airtight container in refrigerator.

# FESTIVE HOLIDAY BARK

16 ounces vanilla-flavored powdered coating
2 cups small pretzel twists
½ cup red and green candy-coated chocolate pieces

Line cookie sheet with waxed paper or parchment paper. Place powdered coating in microwave-safe bowl. Microwave for 2½ minutes. Stir; microwave at 30-second intervals until completely melted and smooth. Place pretzels and candy-coated chocolate pieces in large bowl. Pour melted coating over top and stir until well coated. Spread onto lined baking sheet. Let stand until firm or place in refrigerator to set up faster. Store in container at room temperature.

# OHIO BUCKEYES

1 cup butter or margarine, melted

2 cups peanut butter

4 cups powdered sugar

1 teaspoon vanilla

2 x 2-inch piece of paraffin

3 cups chocolate chips (not imitation chocolate)

Cream together all ingredients except paraffin and chocolate. Chill in refrigerator a few hours, then roll into balls approximately ¾-inch in diameter. Chill the balls in refrigerator at least 8 hours. Melt paraffin and chocolate in double boiler. Using a toothpick, dip each ball into the chocolate mixture, twirling off excess chocolate. Place on waxed paper to set up.

# Choco-Butterscotch Crisps

1 cup butterscotch chips
½ cup peanut butter
4 cups crispy rice cereal
1 cup semisweet chocolate chips

2 tablespoons butter
1 tablespoon water
½ cup powdered sugar

Grease an 8 x 8-inch baking pan. Melt butterscotch chips and peanut butter over very low heat, stirring occasionally. Add cereal and mix well. Press half of mixture into prepared baking pan and chill. Melt chocolate chips, butter, and water in top of double boiler and add powdered sugar. Spread over chilled mixture and press in remainder of cereal mixture. Cut and chill.

# FIVE-MINUTE NEVER-FAIL FUDGE

⅔ cup evaporated milk

1⅓ cups sugar

¼ teaspoon salt

¼ cup butter

16 large marshmallows, cut up

1½ cups semisweet chocolate chips

1 teaspoon vanilla

1 cup walnuts, broken

Grease an 8 x 8-inch baking pan. In a large saucepan, mix together evaporated milk, sugar, salt, butter, and marshmallows; bring to a boil, stirring constantly. Boil for 5 minutes. Remove from heat. Add chocolate chips and stir until melted. Stir in vanilla and walnuts. Spread in prepared baking pan. Cool until firm.

# Chocolate-Drizzled Peanut Butter Fudge

1½ cups sugar
1 cup (5 ounces) evaporated milk
¼ cup butter
1 jar marshmallow creme

1 cup crunchy peanut butter
1 teaspoon vanilla
2 (1 ounce) squares
    semisweet chocolate

Grease an 8 x 8- or 9 x 9-inch baking pan. In a microwave-safe bowl, combine sugar, evaporated milk, and butter. Microwave on high for 6 minutes, stirring halfway through. Cook 4 to 6 minutes more or until small amount of sugar forms soft ball when dropped in water or until temperature reaches 236 degrees. Add remaining ingredients, except chocolate. Beat until well blended. Pour into pan. Cool for 30 minutes. Melt chocolate for 1 to 2 minutes. Stir after 30 seconds. Drizzle over top of fudge.

# MELT-IN-YOUR-MOUTH TOFFEE

2 cups butter or margarine
1 cup sugar
1 cup brown sugar, packed
1 cup walnuts, chopped
2 cups (12 ounces) semisweet chocolate chips

In a heavy saucepan, combine butter and sugars. Cook over medium heat, stirring constantly, until mixture boils. Boil to brittle stage—300 degrees—without stirring. Remove from heat. Pour nuts and chocolate chips into 13 x 9 x 2-inch baking pan. Pour hot mixture over nuts and chocolate. Let mixture cool, and break into pieces before serving.

# ROCKY ROAD CANDY

1 bag semisweet chocolate chips
½ bag colored miniature marshmallows
⅓ cup chopped pecans

Melt chocolate over low heat, or use a double boiler or microwave. Stir in marshmallows and pecans. Spoon onto waxed paper. Form into a log. Refrigerate 2 hours. Slice into ½-inch pieces.

# QUICK CHOCOLATE TRUFFLES

2 (10 to 12 ounce) packages milk chocolate chips
1 (8 ounce) carton frozen whipped topping, thawed
1¼ cups graham cracker crumbs

Line cookie sheets with waxed paper. Microwave chocolate chips on medium-high heat for 1 minute. Stir; microwave 10 to 20 seconds longer until chips are melted. Stir occasionally during melting process. Allow to cool for about 30 minutes; stir occasionally. Fold in whipped topping. Drop rounded teaspoonfuls onto waxed paper-lined cookie sheets. Freeze until firm, about 1½ hours. Shape into balls and roll in crushed graham crackers. Refrigerate in airtight containers. If desired, you may freeze truffles and remove from freezer 30 minutes before serving.

# CARAMEL-COVERED PRETZEL TWISTS

¼ cup semisweet chocolate chips
¼ cup peanut butter chips
2 tablespoons chopped walnuts
1 bag pretzel twists
1 (8 ounce) jar caramel topping

Combine chocolate chips, peanut butter chips, and walnuts in a food processor, crushing into medium chunks. Dip pretzels in caramel and then in the chip and nut mixture. Lay on waxed paper until caramel has thickened.

# CHOCOLATE PEANUT CLUSTERS

2 tablespoons creamy peanut butter
1 cup semisweet chocolate chips
1 cup butterscotch chips
2 cups salted peanuts

In a medium saucepan, combine peanut butter and chocolate and butterscotch chips. Cook over medium heat until chips are melted and smooth. Remove from heat and add peanuts. Drop by rounded spoonfuls onto waxed paper.

# OLD-FASHIONED TAFFY

*Requires two people to make*

1 cup sugar
1 cup dark corn syrup
2 tablespoons water

1 tablespoon apple cider vinegar
1 piece of butter, the size of a peanut
½ teaspoon baking soda

Place first 5 ingredients in a pan; bring to a boil. Boil until mixture forms a hard ball in a cup of cold water. Add baking soda and stir well. Pour into buttered pan. When cool, pull until shiny and ready to cut.

# COOKIE BARK

1 (20 ounce) package chocolate sandwich cookies
2 (18½ ounce) packages white chocolate

Line 10 x 15-inch jellyroll pan with waxed paper. Coat paper with non-stick cooking spray; set aside. Break half of cookies into coarse pieces and place in large bowl. In a microwave-safe bowl, melt one package of white chocolate in microwave. Quickly fold melted chocolate into broken cookie pieces. Pour mixture into prepared pan and spread to cover half of pan. Repeat process with remaining chocolate and cookies. Refrigerate until solid. Remove from pan and carefully peel off waxed paper. Place bark on large cutting board and cut into pieces with a large knife. Store in airtight container.

# CHOCOLATE SNOWBALLS

1¼ cups butter, softened
⅔ cup sugar
1 teaspoon vanilla
2 cups flour

⅛ teaspoon salt
½ cup cocoa
2 cups pecans, chopped
½ cup powdered sugar

In a medium bowl, cream butter and sugar until light and fluffy. Stir in vanilla. Sift together flour, salt, and cocoa; stir into creamed mixture. Mix in pecans until well blended. Cover and chill for at least 2 hours. Preheat oven to 350 degrees. Roll chilled dough into 1-inch balls. Place about 2 inches apart on ungreased cookie sheets. Bake for 20 minutes in preheated oven. Roll in powdered sugar when cooled.

# MOCHA MERINGUE KISSES

*These candies are heart smart!*

3 egg whites
¼ teaspoon cream of tartar
⅔ cup sugar, divided
½ teaspoon vanilla

2 teaspoons cornstarch
1 tablespoon instant coffee
 granules, crushed
¼ cup almonds, finely chopped

Preheat oven to 300 degrees. Beat egg whites with cream of tartar until frothy; gradually add ⅓ cup sugar and beat until stiff. Add vanilla. In separate bowl, mix ⅓ cup sugar with cornstarch, coffee powder, and nuts. Fold in egg white mixture. Spoon onto parchment-lined baking sheets. Bake for 30 minutes. Turn off oven. Allow candies to cool in oven. Tops should be dry and slightly browned.

VARIATION: Use cocoa powder instead of instant coffee.

# PEANUT BUTTER CUPS

2 to 3 pounds melting chocolate
1 cup graham cracker crumbs (7½ whole crackers, crushed)
1 cup butter, melted
¾ cup peanut butter
1 pound powdered sugar

Melt chocolate in double boiler until it is thin and creamy. Coat small paper cup liners with melted chocolate to cup edge; chill. Mix remaining ingredients; add mixture to baking cups and cover with chocolate. Chill until firm.

# Soft Peanut Butter Peanut Brittle

*A softer alternative to a traditional holiday favorite*

2 cups sugar

¼ cup water

1½ cups light corn syrup

2 cups salted peanuts

2 to 2½ cups peanut butter

½ teaspoon vanilla

1½ teaspoons baking soda

Grease a cookie sheet. In a heavy saucepan, combine sugar and water. Bring mixture to full rolling boil over high heat, stirring constantly. Stir in corn syrup. Cook to hard-crack stage—300 degrees. Meanwhile, mix peanuts, peanut butter, and vanilla. Remove syrup from heat; at once add peanut butter mixture and baking soda; stir. Working quickly, pour onto prepared cookie sheet; spread with fork. Cool; break into pieces.

# COOKIES

*Blessed is the season which engages the whole world in a conspiracy of love.*

HAMILTON WRIGHT MABIE

# SOUR CREAM CHRISTMAS COOKIES

1 cup shortening
1 cup butter or margarine
2 cups sugar
2 eggs
2 teaspoons baking soda
¾ teaspoon salt
1 teaspoon baking powder

2 teaspoons vanilla
1 teaspoon lemon juice
1 teaspoon nutmeg
6 cups flour
1 cup sour cream
1 cup buttermilk

Melt shortening and butter together; cream with sugar, eggs, baking soda, salt, and baking powder. Add vanilla, lemon juice, and nutmeg. Alternately add flour, sour cream, and buttermilk. Chill overnight, uncovered. Roll and cut on floured surface. Bake at 375 degrees for 5 to 8 minutes or until soft in middle.

# SOFT MOLASSES COOKIES

1 cup sugar

1 cup molasses

2 heaping teaspoons soda

1 teaspoon salt

1 cup flour

1 cup cold water

1 teaspoon ginger

½ teaspoon cinnamon

½ teaspoon cloves

Preheat oven to 400 degrees. Mix all ingredients together; add enough flour to handle and roll out the dough. Roll thick and cut with a cookie cutter. Bake for approximately 10 minutes.

# Big Chocolate Chip Cookies

1 cup butter or margarine,
   softened
1 cup brown sugar
1 egg
1 teaspoon vanilla
2 cups flour

1 teaspoon baking soda
½ teaspoon salt
1 cup rolled oats
2 cups chocolate chips
½ cup nuts (optional)
½ cup raisins (optional)

Combine butter, brown sugar, egg, and vanilla. Add flour, baking soda, and salt. Add oats, chocolate chips, and, if desired, nuts and raisins; mix well. Measure ¼ cup dough for each cookie, making each cookie 3 inches in diameter and ½ inch thick. Bake at 375 degrees on lightly greased cookie sheets for 15 minutes. Let cool for 5 minutes before removing from sheets.

# OATMEAL COOKIES

4 cups quick-cooking oats
2 cups light brown sugar
1 cup butter or margarine, melted
2 eggs, beaten
1 teaspoon salt
1 teaspoon almond flavoring or ½ teaspoon vanilla
½ cup coconut
½ cup chopped nuts (optional)

Combine all ingredients and refrigerate overnight. Drop by rounded teaspoons onto greased cookie sheet. Bake at 350 degrees for 10 minutes.

# ANGEL COOKIES

1 cup sugar
1 cup butter or margarine, softened
1 egg
1 teaspoon vanilla
½ teaspoon almond extract
2 cups flour
½ teaspoon baking soda
½ teaspoon cream of tartar
¼ teaspoon salt
Water
Sugar

Preheat oven to 375 degrees. Beat together sugar and butter at medium speed until creamy. Add egg, vanilla, and almond extract, beating well. Reduce speed and add flour, baking soda, cream of tartar, and salt. Shape dough into 1-inch balls. Dip top of each ball in water, then in sugar. Place the balls on an ungreased cookie sheet, 2 inches apart. Bake for 7 to 9 minutes. Makes about 3 dozen cookies.

# CHUNKY PEANUT BUTTER CHOCOLATE CHIP COOKIE MIX

¼ cup sugar

½ cup chopped salted peanuts

¾ cup packed brown sugar chunks

1¾ cups flour

¾ teaspoon baking soda

½ teaspoon salt

½ cup semisweet chocolate

½ cup milk chocolate chips

In a 1-quart glass jar, layer ingredients in order given, combining flour, baking soda, and salt. Attach a recipe card with the following instructions on page 115.

# CHUNKY PEANUT BUTTER CHOCOLATE CHIP COOKIES

**Chunky Peanut Butter Chocolate Chip Cookie Mix**
¾ cup chunky peanut butter
½ cup butter, softened
1 egg
1 tablespoon vanilla

Preheat oven to 375 degrees. Carefully remove milk chocolate chips and semisweet chocolate chunks from Chunky Peanut Butter Chocolate Chip Cookie Mix; set aside. In a large mixing bowl, empty remaining contents of cookie mix, stirring well to combine. Add peanut butter, butter, egg, and vanilla. Beat with an electric mixer until well blended. Add chocolate chips and chunks, stirring to combine. Drop by rounded tablespoonfuls 2 inches apart onto an ungreased cookie sheet. Bake for 10 to 12 minutes or until lightly browned. Cool 2 minutes on cookie sheet before removing to a wire rack.

# VELVET CUTOUT COOKIES

2 cups butter, softened
1 (8 ounce) package cream cheese, softened
2 cups sugar
2 egg yolks
2 teaspoons vanilla
4½ cups flour
¼ teaspoon salt

In a large mixing bowl, cream together butter, cream cheese, and sugar until light and fluffy. Add egg yolks and vanilla; mix well. Gradually stir in flour and salt. Chill for 2 hours. Roll out dough on floured surface and cut into desired shapes. Place on greased baking sheets and bake at 350 degrees for 9 to 12 minutes. Cool on cookie sheets before removing to wire racks. Frost if desired.

FROSTING:
4 tablespoons butter, softened
1 (3 ounce) package cream cheese, softened
3 cups powdered sugar, divided
3 tablespoons milk
½ teaspoon vanilla
Food coloring (optional)

In a mixing bowl, beat together butter, cream cheese, and 1 cup powdered sugar until smooth. Add milk and vanilla. Gradually mix in remaining powdered sugar and beat until smooth and spreadable. Divide frosting and tint with food coloring if desired.

# CARAMEL BROWNIES

| | |
|---|---|
| 2 cups sugar | 1 teaspoon salt |
| ¾ cup cocoa | 1 teaspoon baking powder |
| 1 cup oil | 1 cup semisweet chocolate chips |
| 4 eggs | 1 cup walnuts, chopped, divided |
| ¼ cup milk | 1 (14 ounce) package caramels |
| 1½ cups flour | 1 (14 ounce) can sweetened condensed milk |

Preheat oven to 350 degrees. In a mixing bowl, combine sugar, cocoa, oil, eggs, and milk. Combine flour, salt, and baking powder; add to egg mixture and mix well. Fold in chocolate chips and ½ cup walnuts. Spoon two-thirds of batter into greased 13 x 9 x 2-inch baking pan. Bake for 12 minutes. Meanwhile, in a saucepan, heat caramels and condensed milk over low heat until caramels are melted. Pour over baked brownie layer. Sprinkle with remaining walnuts. Drop remaining batter by teaspoonfuls over caramel layer; carefully swirl brownie batter with a knife. Bake 35 to 40 minutes longer or until toothpick inserted near center comes out with moist crumbs. Cool on wire rack.

# BON-BON CHRISTMAS COOKIES

4 ounces cream cheese, softened
½ cup butter-flavored shortening
2 cups flour, sifted
Water
1½ cups powdered sugar, sifted
2 (10 ounce) jars stemless maraschino cherries, drained

In a medium bowl, stir together cream cheese and shortening until well blended. Stir in flour, using your hands, if needed, to help form dough. If mixture seems too dry, add 1 to 2 teaspoons water. Cover and chill several hours or overnight. Preheat oven to 375 degrees. Lightly grease cookie sheets. Before rolling out dough, dust rolling surface heavily with powdered sugar. Roll out dough to ⅛-inch thickness. Cut into 1 x 4-inch strips. Place cherry on end of each strip. Roll up each strip starting with cherry. Place on prepared cookie sheets and dust with powdered sugar. Bake for 7 to 10 minutes in preheated oven. Cookies should brown slightly. After baking, dust again with powdered sugar. Allow cookies to cool before serving, as cherries are very hot!

# APPLESAUCE JUMBLES

2 eggs
½ cup shortening
1½ cups brown sugar
1 teaspoon vanilla
¾ cup applesauce
2 cups flour
1 teaspoon salt

½ teaspoon baking soda
1 teaspoon cinnamon
¼ teaspoon mace
¼ teaspoon cloves
1 cup raisins
1 cup nuts, chopped

Cream eggs, shortening, brown sugar, and vanilla. Mix in applesauce. Add remaining ingredients and mix well. Cover and chill 2 hours. Drop rounded teaspoonfuls on ungreased cookie sheet. Bake at 375 degrees for 10 minutes or until there is no indentation when touched. Remove and cool before frosting.

# TRIPLE CHOCOLATE CHUNK COOKIE MIX

½ cup sugar

¾ cup brown sugar, packed

1¾ cups flour

1 teaspoon baking soda

½ teaspoon salt

⅓ cup unsweetened cocoa powder

4 ounces white chocolate chunks

½ cup milk chocolate chips

⅓ cup semisweet chocolate chips

In a 1-quart glass jar, layer ingredients in order given, combining flour, baking soda, and salt. Attach a recipe card with the following instructions on page 121.

# TRIPLE CHOCOLATE CHUNK COOKIES

**Triple Chocolate Chunk Cookie Mix**
1 cup butter, softened
1 teaspoon vanilla
2 eggs

Preheat oven to 325 degrees. Carefully remove semisweet chocolate chips, milk chocolate chips, and white chocolate chunks from Triple Chocolate Chunk Cookie Mix; set aside. In a mixing bowl, beat butter, vanilla, and eggs until creamy. In a large bowl, empty remaining contents of cookie mix, stirring to combine; add to creamed mixture until well blended. Stir in chocolate chips and white chocolate chunks. Drop by rounded tablespoonfuls onto an ungreased cookie sheet. Bake for 11 to 13 minutes or until cookies are set and appear dry. Cool 1 minute on cookie sheet before removing to a wire rack.

# CHEWY CHOCOLATE COOKIES

½ cup shortening
1 cup sugar
1 large egg
1 teaspoon vanilla
1¾ cups flour
½ teaspoon baking soda

¼ teaspoon salt
½ cup cocoa
½ cup milk
½ cup chopped pecans
24 large marshmallows, cut in half
Pecan halves

Chocolate Frosting:
2 cups sifted powdered sugar
¼ cup plus 1 tablespoon cocoa
3 tablespoons butter, softened
¼ cup milk

Preheat oven to 350 degrees. In a large bowl, beat shortening on medium speed. Gradually add sugar. Beat well. Add egg and vanilla and again beat well. In a separate bowl, combine flour, soda, salt, and cocoa. Slowly add to shortening mixture alternately with milk. When alternating, begin and end with flour mixture, being sure to mix well after each addition. Finally stir in chopped pecans. Drop dough by rounded teaspoonfuls onto lightly greased cookie sheets. Bake for 8 minutes. After cookies have baked for 8 minutes, remove from oven. Place a marshmallow half, cut side down, on top of each cookie. Bake 2 minutes more. Remove to wire racks. Allow to cool completely before spreading with chocolate frosting and topping with a pecan half. To prepare chocolate frosting, combine all frosting ingredients. Beat on medium speed until light and fluffy.

# CHOCOLATE CRINKLES

1 cup cocoa

2 cups sugar

2 teaspoons vanilla

½ teaspoon salt

½ cup oil

4 eggs

2 cups flour

2 teaspoons baking powder

Powdered sugar

Combine first 8 ingredients, mixing well. Refrigerate overnight. Form balls and roll in powdered sugar. Bake at 350 degrees for 10 to 12 minutes. Sprinkle with powdered sugar after baking if desired.

# CHOCOLATE MINT BROWNIE MIX

2 cups sugar
¾ cup unsweetened cocoa powder
1 cup flour
¾ teaspoon salt
1 teaspoon baking powder
1 cup chopped chocolate mint wafers

In a 1-quart glass jar, layer ingredients in order given, combining flour, salt, and baking powder. Attach a recipe card with the following instructions:

# CHOCOLATE MINT BROWNIES

Chocolate Mint Brownie Mix
1 cup butter, softened
3 eggs, slightly beaten
1½ teaspoons vanilla

Preheat oven to 350 degrees. Grease and flour a 13 x 9 x 2-inch baking pan. In a large mixing bowl, empty contents of Chocolate Mint Brownie Mix, stirring to combine. Add butter, eggs, and vanilla. Beat with a spoon until well blended. Spread batter into prepared pan. Bake for 35 to 40 minutes or until toothpick inserted near center comes out clean. Cool in pan on a wire rack. Cut into squares.

# BEST DATE COOKIES

1 cup brown sugar

⅔ cup butter or ⅓ cup butter and ⅓ cup shortening

1 egg

1 teaspoon salt

1 teaspoon baking soda

¼ cup milk

2 cups flour

1 cup dates, chopped

½ cup nuts, chopped

Preheat oven to 375 degrees. Mix together all ingredients and drop onto ungreased cookie sheets. Bake for 15 minutes.

# CHRISTMAS EVE COOKIES

1 cup sugar
½ cup butter
½ cup shortening
1 egg, separated

2 cups flour
½ teaspoon salt
1½ tablespoons cinnamon
1½ cups chopped nuts

Preheat oven to 350 degrees. Grease and flour a 10 x 15-inch pan. In a mixing bowl, cream sugar, butter, and shortening. Add egg yolk and dry ingredients. Press into pan. Beat egg white until foamy and spread very thinly over batter. Press on nuts. Bake for about 30 minutes. Cut into squares and serve.

# Easy Gingerbread Cutouts

1 box spice cake mix
¾ cup flour
2 eggs
⅓ cup oil
⅓ cup molasses
2 teaspoons ginger
¾ cup canned cream cheese frosting, warmed slightly
Red-hot candies or other small decorative candies

Combine cake mix, flour, eggs, oil, molasses, and ginger. Mix thoroughly. Refrigerate for 30 minutes or until dough is easily handled. Preheat oven to 375 degrees. On a floured board, roll dough to ⅛-inch thickness. Cut with 5-inch cookie cutters that have been dipped in flour. Place 3 inches apart on ungreased baking sheets. Bake for 7 to 10 minutes or until edges are firm and bottom is lightly browned. Cool on wire racks. Decorate with cream cheese frosting and candies, as desired.

# CHEWY CHOCOLATE BARS

2 cups semisweet chocolate chips
1 (14 ounce) can sweetened condensed milk
¾ cup butter, softened
1¼ cups brown sugar, packed
2 eggs
1½ cups flour
¾ cup rolled oats
½ teaspoon salt

Preheat oven to 350 degrees. In a saucepan, melt chocolate chips with milk over low heat; set aside. In a bowl, cream butter and brown sugar until soft; beat in eggs. Blend flour, rolled oats, and salt into creamed mixture. Spread half of batter into greased 13 x 9 x 2-inch baking pan. Spread chocolate mixture on top of batter. Spread remaining batter over chocolate layer. Bake for 35 minutes. Cool and cut into bars.

# PEANUT BUTTER CHOCOLATE KISS COOKIES

½ cup shortening

¾ cup peanut butter

⅓ cup sugar

⅓ cup brown sugar, packed

1 egg

2 tablespoons milk

1 teaspoon vanilla

1⅓ cups flour

1 teaspoon baking soda

½ teaspoon salt

Sugar

1 cup (6 ounces) chocolate kisses

Preheat oven to 375 degrees. Cream shortening and peanut butter. Add sugars, egg, milk, and vanilla. Beat well. In large mixing bowl, combine flour, baking soda, and salt. Gradually add creamed mixture to flour mixture and blend thoroughly. Shape dough into 1-inch balls; roll in sugar. Place on ungreased cookie sheet. Bake for 10 to 12 minutes. Remove from oven immediately and place unwrapped kiss on top of each cookie. Remove from cookie sheet and cool.

# RICH CHOCOLATE FUDGE BROWNIE MIX

2 cups flour
1 teaspoon baking soda
1 cup brown sugar, packed
⅓ cup unsweetened cocoa powder
1 cup sugar
1½ cups semisweet chocolate chips

Combine flour and baking soda. Place in bottom of a 1-quart glass jar. Layer remaining ingredients in order given. Attach a recipe card with the following instructions:

# RICH CHOCOLATE FUDGE BROWNIES

Rich Chocolate Fudge Brownie Mix
1 cup butter, softened
2 eggs
1 teaspoon vanilla
1½ cups buttermilk

Preheat oven to 400 degrees. Grease and flour a 13 x 9 x 2-inch baking pan. In a large mixing bowl, empty contents of Rich Chocolate Fudge Brownie Mix, stirring well to combine. Add butter, eggs, vanilla, and buttermilk. Beat until well blended. Spread batter into prepared pan. Bake for 35 to 40 minutes or until toothpick inserted near center comes out clean.

# DESSERTS

*Until one feels the spirit of Christmas, there is no Christmas. All else is outward display—so much tinsel and decorations. For it isn't the holly, it isn't the snow. It isn't the tree nor the firelight's glow. It's the warmth that comes to the hearts of men when the Christmas spirit returns again.*

UNKNOWN

# CHOCOLATE ALMOND PIE

½ cup milk
16 large marshmallows
6 chocolate-almond candy bars
1 cup whipping cream, whipped
1 (9 inch) piecrust, baked and cooled
Sweetened whipped cream
Chocolate curls

In a saucepan, heat milk until hot; dissolve marshmallows in hot milk. Break and add candy bars. Stir until melted. Remove from heat and cool. Fold in 1 cup whipped cream. Pour into baked 9-inch piecrust. Refrigerate until set. Serve with sweetened whipped cream and chocolate curls.

# SNICKERDOODLE CAKE

1 German chocolate cake mix
1 (14 ounce) package caramels
½ cup butter or margarine
⅓ cup milk
¾ cup semisweet chocolate chips
1 cup walnuts, chopped

Preheat oven to 350 degrees. Prepare cake mix according to package directions. Pour half of batter into greased 13 x 9 x 2-inch baking pan. Bake for 20 minutes. In a saucepan, melt caramels with butter and milk over low heat, stirring frequently. Pour over baked cake. Sprinkle with chocolate chips and nuts. Spoon remaining cake batter over caramel layer. Bake at 250 degrees for 20 minutes. Increase temperature to 350 degrees and bake for an additional 10 minutes.

# CHOCOLATE CHIP CHEESECAKE

1½ cups chocolate sandwich cookie crumbs

3 tablespoons butter, melted

3 (8 ounce) packages cream cheese, softened

1 (14 ounce) can sweetened condensed milk

2 teaspoons vanilla

3 eggs

1 cup semisweet chocolate chips, divided

1 teaspoon flour

Preheat oven to 300 degrees. Combine cookie crumbs and butter; press into 9-inch springform pan. Beat cream cheese until fluffy, then beat in milk, vanilla, and eggs; set aside. In a separate bowl, toss ½ cup chocolate chips with flour to coat; stir into cream cheese mixture. Pour batter into prepared pan; sprinkle with remaining chips. Bake for 1 hour or until cake springs back when lightly touched. Cool. Chill. Serve.

# MOTHER'S APPLE CAKE

2 cups sugar
¾ cup oil
1 teaspoon salt
1 teaspoon vanilla
2 large eggs
2½ cups flour
1 teaspoon baking soda, mixed into flour

3 cups diced apples
1 cup chopped nuts
1 teaspoon cinnamon
½ cup raisins (optional)
Whipped topping (optional)

SAUCE:
1 cup brown sugar
½ cup heavy cream

¼ cup butter
½ teaspoon cinnamon

Preheat oven to 350 degrees. Mix sugar and oil well. Add salt, vanilla, and eggs. Cream well. Add flour, baking soda, apples, nuts, cinnamon, and raisins. Spread into a 13 x 9 x 2-inch pan. Bake for 50 to 60 minutes. When cake is nearly done, mix all sauce ingredients in a saucepan. Bring to a boil and remove from heat. Pour sauce over hot cake. If desired, serve cake with whipped topping.

# CHOCOLATE CHIFFON CAKE

2 cups hot water
⅔ cup cocoa
2 cups flour
4 teaspoons baking powder
½ teaspoon baking soda
1 teaspoon salt

2 cups sugar
½ cup oil
1 teaspoon vanilla
6 eggs, separated
½ teaspoon cream of tartar

Preheat oven to 350 degrees. In a saucepan, combine hot water and cocoa. Boil for 1 minute. Cool. In a separate bowl, sift flour, baking powder, baking soda, salt, and sugar. Add cooled cocoa syrup, oil, vanilla, and egg yolks. Blend until smooth. In a separate bowl, beat egg whites and cream of tartar until very stiff. Carefully fold egg whites into first mixture. Bake in ungreased tube pan for approximately 50 minutes.

COCOA FROSTING:
1½ cups cold milk
1 envelope whipped topping mix
1 (4-serving size) package chocolate fudge instant pudding

Pour cold milk in mixing bowl; add contents of whipped topping envelope and pudding mix. Beat on low for 1 minute. Slowly increase speed and beat for 4 to 6 minutes. Allow cake to cool completely before frosting.

# ANY FRUIT OR BERRY PIE

Fruit or berries, fresh or frozen (enough to fill piecrust)
¾ cup sugar
2 cups water
2 tablespoons cornstarch
Pinch salt
1 small package gelatin, same flavor as fruit
1 (9 inch) piecrust, baked and cooled
1 small container frozen whipped topping, thawed

Drain berries, pat dry, and sprinkle with sugar. Set aside. In a saucepan, mix water, cornstarch, and salt. Bring to a boil; add gelatin and mix until dissolved. Continue to boil until syrupy. Remove from heat and let cool until right consistency to add fruit or berries. Gelatin mixture should be set enough to prevent fruit from sinking and cool enough to prevent fruit from cooking. Pour into piecrust. Chill completely. Top with whipped topping. Serve.

# WHIPPED CREAM CAKE

1½ cups butter, softened
3 cups sugar
6 eggs

3 cups flour
½ pint whipping cream

Preheat oven to 300 degrees. Cream butter and sugar. Add eggs, one at a time, beating after each addition. Beginning and ending with flour, alternately add flour and cream. (Do not whip cream.) Lightly grease and flour a tube pan. Pour mixture into pan and bake for 2 hours.

# CHOCOLATE PEANUT BUTTER PIE

2 cups extra crunchy peanut butter
1 (8 ounce) package fat-free cream cheese, softened
2 cups powdered sugar
1 cup skim milk
3 (8 ounce) containers frozen whipped topping, thawed
3 (9 inch) prepared chocolate crumb piecrusts

Mix peanut butter and cream cheese until smooth. Add powdered sugar, milk, and 12 ounces (1½ containers) whipped topping. Blend thoroughly and pour into piecrusts, spreading evenly. Top each pie with 4 ounces whipped topping. (These pies freeze and keep well.) For added freshness, store pies in 1-gallon freezer bags.

# CHOCOLATE CHIP ROCKY ROAD PIE

½ cup butter
1 cup dark brown sugar, packed
1 egg, slightly beaten
2 tablespoons hot water
1 teaspoon vanilla
1 cup flour, sifted
½ teaspoon baking powder

¼ teaspoon salt
⅛ teaspoon baking soda
½ cup nuts, chopped
1 cup mini semisweet chocolate chips, divided
1 cup miniature marshmallows, divided

Preheat oven to 350 degrees. In a saucepan, melt butter over low heat; mix in brown sugar until well blended. Add egg, hot water, and vanilla. In a separate bowl, stir together flour, baking powder, salt, and baking soda. Add to sugar mixture; mix well. Mix in nuts, half of chocolate chips, and half of marshmallows. Spread mixture into two 9-inch pie plates; sprinkle with remaining chips and marshmallows. Bake for 20 minutes. Cool.

# PUMPKIN PECAN PIE

1 (15 ounce) can pumpkin
1 cup sugar
½ cup dark corn syrup
1 teaspoon vanilla
1 cup pecans, halved

½ teaspoon cinnamon
¼ teaspoon salt
3 eggs
1 (9 inch) piecrust,
    unbaked

Preheat oven to 350 degrees. In a large mixing bowl, blend together first 7 ingredients. Add eggs and mix well. Pour into unbaked piecrust and top with additional pecans. Bake for 40 to 50 minutes or until knife inserted 1 inch from edge of pie comes out clean.

# Pumpkin Pie Dessert Squares

1 box yellow cake mix, divided
1 egg

½ cup butter or margarine,
    melted

FILLING:

3 cups (1 pound 14 ounce can)
    pumpkin pie mix

2 eggs
⅔ cup milk

TOPPING:

1 cup reserved cake mix
¼ cup sugar
1 tablespoon cinnamon

¼ cup butter, softened
    to room temperature

Preheat oven to 350 degrees. Grease bottom only of 13 x 9 x 2-inch pan. Reserve 1 cup of the cake mix for topping. Combine remaining cake mix, egg, and melted butter. Press into bottom of pan. Mix filling ingredients until smooth and pour over bottom layer. Mix topping ingredients and sprinkle over the top of filling. Bake for 40 to 45 minutes or until knife inserted in the middle comes out clean. If desired, serve with whipped topping. For more of a cinnamon flavor, you may increase the amount of sugar and cinnamon in the topping.

# CHRISTMAS CRUNCH

2 cups sugar
⅔ cup light corn syrup
½ cup water
3 tablespoons butter

1 teaspoon vanilla
½ teaspoon baking soda
2 cups crispy rice cereal
1 cup cashews

Grease a 10 x 15-inch baking pan. In a large saucepan over medium heat, combine sugar, corn syrup, and water; bring to a boil, stirring constantly, until sugar is dissolved. Continue to cook, without stirring, until candy thermometer reads 300 degrees. Remove from heat; stir in butter, vanilla, and baking soda. Add cereal and cashews; pour into prepared pan and allow to cool. Break into pieces and store in airtight container.

# Southern Pecan Pie

Single Crust Plain Pastry:

| | |
|---|---|
| 1 cup flour | 6 tablespoons shortening |
| ½ teaspoon salt | 2 to 3 tablespoons very cold water |

Filling:

| | |
|---|---|
| 1 cup brown sugar, firmly packed | 2 tablespoons butter, melted |
| 1 cup light corn syrup | ⅛ teaspoon salt |
| 4 eggs | 1 cup pecan halves |

Preheat oven to 375 degrees. Prepare single crust pastry by spooning flour into dry measuring cup. Pour flour into mixing bowl and add salt. Stir to blend. Cut in half of shortening until mixture resembles coarse cornmeal. Cut in remaining shortening until crumbles are pea-sized. Add water, a little at a time, with fork. Shape dough into firm ball. Roll out on lightly floured surface. Place loosely in a 9-inch pie dish. Dough should be 1 inch wider than dish. Fold edge under. Moisten rim of pan. Flute edges of pastry. Prepare filling by combining all ingredients except pecans. Beat with rotary beater until smooth. Pour into unbaked pastry. Sprinkle with pecan halves. Bake for 40 to 45 minutes.

# CHOCOLATE TURTLE CHEESECAKE

1 (7 ounce) package caramels
¼ cup evaporated milk
½ cup pecans, chopped
1 (9 inch) prepared chocolate crumb piecrust
2 (3 ounce) packages cream cheese, softened
½ cup sour cream
1¼ cups milk
1 (3.9 ounce) package chocolate instant pudding
½ cup fudge topping
¼ cup pecans, chopped

Place caramels and evaporated milk in large saucepan. Heat over medium heat, stirring constantly, until smooth. Stir in ½ cup pecans. Pour into piecrust. Combine cream cheese, sour cream, milk, and pudding mix in blender. Process until smooth. Pour pudding mixture over caramel layer, covering evenly. Loosely cover pie and chill until set. Drizzle fudge topping over pudding layer in decorative pattern. Sprinkle with ¼ cup pecans. Cover loosely and chill in refrigerator.

# MILK CHOCOLATE POPCORN

12 cups popcorn, popped
2½ cups salted peanuts
1 cup light corn syrup
1 (11.5 ounce) package milk chocolate chips
¼ cup butter or margarine

Preheat oven to 300 degrees. Grease large roasting pan. Line large bowl or serving plate with waxed paper. Combine popcorn and nuts in prepared roasting pan. Combine corn syrup, morsels, and butter in medium heavy-duty saucepan. Cook over medium heat, stirring constantly, until mixture boils. Pour over popcorn; toss well to coat. Bake, stirring frequently, for 30 to 40 minutes. Cool slightly in pan; transfer to prepared serving plate. Store in airtight container for up to two weeks.

# BANANA SPLIT PIE

1 (3.9 ounce) package vanilla instant pudding

1¼ cups cold milk

1 (12 ounce) container frozen whipped topping, thawed and divided

2 bananas, sliced into ¼-inch slices, divided

1 (9 inch) prepared chocolate crumb crust

1 (12 ounce) jar hot fudge topping

1 (20 ounce) can pineapple chunks, drained

12 maraschino cherries with stems, drained

3 tablespoons walnut pieces

In a large bowl, stir together pudding mix and milk. Beat until smooth and thick. Fold in 2 cups whipped topping and one sliced banana. Reserve one half of the banana pudding mixture and spread remainder into piecrust. Reserve 3 tablespoons hot fudge topping for drizzling on top. Gently spread half of the remaining hot fudge topping over banana pudding in piecrust. Repeat layers with remaining banana pudding and fudge topping. Refrigerate for 1 hour or until firm. Arrange pineapple chunks in single layer on top of pie. Spread with remaining whipped topping, swirling topping into peaks with back of spoon. Refrigerate for 30 minutes. Heat reserved fudge topping in microwave until hot enough to pour. Using a fork, drizzle topping over pie. Garnish with maraschino cherries and walnut pieces.

# BANANA PUDDING PIE

2 bananas, sliced
1 Oreo piecrust
1 (3⅛ ounce) box French vanilla instant pudding
1 (8 ounce) container frozen whipped topping, thawed
Crushed Oreos (optional)

Place sliced bananas in bottom of piecrust. Prepare pudding according to package directions. Pour pudding over bananas. Allow to set. When pudding is set, top with whipped topping. Garnish with crushed Oreos, if desired. Refrigerate until ready to serve.

# CHERRY CHRISTMAS DESSERT

1 (21 ounce) can cherry pie filling
1 (8 ounce) container frozen whipped topping, thawed
1 (14 ounce) can sweetened condensed milk
1 (10 ounce) can crushed pineapple, drained
1 package cherry gelatin
½ cup nuts, chopped

Combine all ingredients in a large bowl; mix well. Refrigerate for at least 4 hours before serving.

# VERY BERRY PIE

Pastry for a double crust, 9-inch pie
1 cup sugar
⅓ cup flour
5 cups mixed berries (blueberries, raspberries, and sliced strawberries)*
1 tablespoon lemon juice
1 tablespoon butter

Prepare desired pastry and divide in half. Roll out one portion to fit a 9-inch pie plate. Place in plate and trim edges evenly. In a bowl, combine sugar and flour. Add berries and lemon juice. Toss berries to completely coat. Transfer berry mixture to pastry-lined pie plate. Dot berry mixture with butter. Roll remaining pastry into a 12-inch circle. Place on top of pie filling. Cut slits to vent. Trim dough to ½ inch beyond pie plate. Fold top of pastry under bottom pastry. Seal and flute edges. Place pie on baking sheet. Bake at 375 degrees for 50 minutes or until pie is done.

NOTE: *If you choose to use frozen berries, toss them with sugar mixture while frozen. Allow to sit 15 to 30 minutes or until partially thawed before transferring them to crust-lined plate.*

# TAPIOCA PUDDING FOR THE HOLIDAYS

3 heaping tablespoons
   large round tapioca
¾ cup water
4 cups milk
3 eggs, separated
1 cup sugar

1 teaspoon salt
1 teaspoon vanilla
¼ cup sugar
Pinch salt
Red and green sugars

In a covered dish, soak tapioca in water overnight. In the morning, add tapioca to milk and cook in a heavy kettle very slowly over low heat until tapioca is clear. Beat egg yolks with 1 cup of sugar and 1 teaspoon of salt. Slowly add to milk mixture. Cook a little longer, and then add vanilla. Pour into a large casserole dish. Whip egg whites until stiff. Add ¼ cup sugar and a pinch of salt. Place meringue over pudding and brown in a 300-degree oven. Cook slowly until done, but check often to prevent burning. Sprinkle with red and green sugars.

# GRANNY'S SUGAR CREAM PIE

¾ cup sugar, granulated
4 tablespoons flour
2 cups half-and-half
Dash salt

1 (9 inch) unbaked pie shell
1 tablespoon butter
Dash nutmeg

Mix sugar, flour, half-and-half, and salt in unbaked pie shell, using fingertips. Add more flour if it looks soupy. Dot with butter and sprinkle with nutmeg. Bake at 350 degrees for 45 to 60 minutes. Pie will thicken as it cools.

# JELLY ROLL

3 eggs
1 cup sugar
⅓ cup water
1 teaspoon vanilla
¾ cup flour

1 teaspoon baking powder
¼ teaspoon salt
Powdered sugar
¾ cup raspberry jam
   or preserves

Heat oven to 375 degrees. Line roll pan with aluminum foil. In small bowl, beat eggs about 5 minutes until very thick. Pour eggs into a larger mixing bowl; gradually add sugar. Blend in water and vanilla on low. Gradually add flour, baking powder, and salt. Beat until batter is smooth. Pour into pan, spreading batter into corners. Bake 12 to 15 minutes. Loosen cake from edges, invert on towel, and sprinkle with powdered sugar.

Carefully remove foil; trim off any hard edges if needed. While hot, roll cake and towel from narrow end. Cool on wire rack. Unroll cake; remove towel. Beat jam or preserves to soften, and spread over cake. Roll and sprinkle with powdered sugar.

# DIRT CAKE

1 (16 ounce) package chocolate sandwich cookies
1 (8 ounce) package cream cheese, softened
½ cup butter, softened
1 cup powdered sugar
1 (8 ounce) container frozen whipped topping, thawed
2 (3 ounce) packages vanilla instant pudding
3 cups milk
1 teaspoon vanilla

Crush cookies and put half of crumbs in 13 x 9 x 2-inch baking pan.
Mix cream cheese and butter until smooth. Mix in powdered sugar.
Fold in whipped topping. In a separate bowl, mix pudding mixes, milk,
and vanilla. Fold in cream cheese mixture. Stir well. Pour batter on top
of crumbs. Sprinkle remaining crumbs on top. Refrigerate.

# MAIN DISHES

Joy to the world, the Lord is come!
Let earth receive her King;
Let every heart prepare Him room,
And Heaven and nature sing,
And Heaven and nature sing,
And Heaven, and Heaven, and nature sing.

ISAAC WATTS

# ROAST BEEF AND POTATOES

1 beef roast, any cut

2 garlic cloves, thinly sliced

1 teaspoon thyme

1½ teaspoons pepper, divided

3 tablespoons olive oil

7 small red potatoes,
    cut into chunks

½ cup beef broth

Cut small slits in beef. Stuff each slit with one garlic slice. Mix thyme
and 1 teaspoon of the pepper. Rub thyme mixture over beef. Place oil
in Dutch oven and brown beef on all sides. Toss remaining pepper with
potatoes. Add to the Dutch oven. Pour broth over meat and potatoes.
Cover and bake at 300 degrees for 4 hours or until tender.

# BAKED SPAGHETTI

1 (8 ounce) box spaghetti, cooked and drained
1 pound ground beef, browned and drained
1 cup mozzarella cheese, shredded
1 jar spaghetti sauce

Mix together spaghetti, ground beef, and cheese. Add sauce. Spray casserole dish with cooking spray. Put mixture in dish and cover with additional shredded cheese if desired. Bake at 250 degrees for 35 to 40 minutes.

# BAKED CORNISH GAME HENS

4 Cornish game hens
½ cup butter, softened
1 teaspoon sage

2 cloves garlic, pressed
2 tablespoons lemon juice

Preheat oven to 350 degrees. Remove neck and giblets from hens. Rinse and pat dry. Rub hens with butter. In a small bowl, combine sage, garlic, and lemon juice. Place hens in roasting pan and bake for 1 hour, basting with lemon mixture every 10 minutes.

# Buttermilk Baked Cod

1½ pounds cod fillets
½ cup butter, melted
1 teaspoon salt
1 teaspoon paprika

1 teaspoon garlic powder
1 teaspoon lemon juice
1 cup buttermilk
2 cups herb-seasoned stuffing mix

Rinse and dry cod fillets; cut into serving pieces. Melt butter; add salt, paprika, garlic powder, and lemon juice. Dip fish in buttermilk; roll in stuffing. Place in foil-lined 13 x 9 x 2-inch baking pan. Drizzle butter mixture over fish. Bake at 450 degrees for 10 to 15 minutes.

# BEEF STEW

2 tablespoons oil
2 pounds beef stew meat
   (use venison if you prefer)
3 large onions, coarsely chopped
2 garlic cloves, crushed
1 tablespoon Worcestershire sauce
1 bay leaf
1 teaspoon oregano

1 tablespoon salt
1 teaspoon pepper
7 potatoes, peeled and quartered
1 pound carrots, peeled and cut
   into 1-inch pieces
¼ cup flour
¼ cup cold water
Bottled browning sauce (optional)

Heat oil in a large Dutch oven. Brown all sides of meat. Add onions, garlic, Worcestershire sauce, bay leaf, oregano, salt, and pepper. Simmer, covered, 1½ to 2 hours or until meat is tender. Add vegetables. Cook until vegetables are tender, 30 to 45 minutes. Mix flour and water; stir mixture into stew. Cook and stir stew until thickened and bubbly. If you would like additional color, add browning sauce. Remove and discard bay leaf. Serve.

# SWISS STEAK AND POTATOES

5 cups small red potatoes, thinly sliced
1 large onion, chopped
1 small clove garlic, minced
1 pound beef top round steak, trimmed of all fat
    and diagonally cut into 1-inch strips
1 (15 ounce) can reduced-sodium tomato sauce
⅓ cup ketchup
1 tablespoon brown sugar, packed
1 tablespoon cider vinegar
½ teaspoon thyme
¼ teaspoon salt
⅛ teaspoon pepper
1 large bay leaf

Combine potatoes, onion, and garlic in a 2½-quart microwave-safe casserole dish. Microwave on high power for 5 to 6 minutes or until potatoes are partially cooked. Stir after 3 minutes. Lightly coat a Dutch oven with nonstick cooking spray. Add meat. Sauté over medium heat until meat is browned. Stir in tomato sauce, ketchup, brown sugar, vinegar, thyme, salt, pepper, and bay leaf. Stir in the potato mixture. Bring to a boil; reduce heat. Cover and simmer for 25 to 30 minutes or until meat is tender. Remove and discard bay leaf. Serve immediately.

# DR. PEPPER GLAZED HAM

1 (2 liter) bottle Dr. Pepper, divided
1 tablespoon ground cloves
1 teaspoon cinnamon
1 fully-cooked ham,
    7 to 10 pound
Whole cloves

Place ham in roasting pan
and cover with mixture
of Dr. Pepper and spices.
Bake ham for 1½ hours at
325 degrees oven. Remove
from oven and score top of ham. Stud ham with cloves.

Mix together:
1 teaspoon cinnamon
1 teaspoon dry mustard

Add enough Dr. Pepper to form a paste. Brush mixture over scored ham.

Mix together:
1 cup brown sugar
¼ cup Dr. Pepper or enough to form a paste

Brush final mixture over ham. Bake an additional 1½ hours or until ham reaches an internal temperature of 140 degrees.

# CRANBERRY CHICKEN

6 boneless, skinless chicken
    breast halves
1 can whole-berry cranberry sauce
1 large Granny Smith apple,
    peeled and diced

½ cup raisins
1 teaspoon orange zest
¼ cup chopped walnuts
1 teaspoon curry powder
1 teaspoon cinnamon

Preheat oven to 350 degrees. Place chicken in greased 13 x 9 x 2-inch baking dish. Bake for 20 minutes. While chicken is cooking, combine remaining ingredients. Spoon cranberry mixture over chicken. Return to oven for 20 to 25 minutes or until chicken juices run clear.

# CAVATINI

1 pound ground beef
⅛ teaspoon garlic powder
1 onion, chopped
1 green pepper, chopped
1 package sliced pepperoni
1 small can mushrooms, drained
32 ounces spaghetti sauce
½ pound curly noodles, cooked and drained
½ pound mozzarella cheese, shredded

Brown ground beef; add garlic powder, onion, and green pepper. Cook until tender, then drain. Stir in pepperoni, mushrooms, and spaghetti sauce. Grease 13 x 9 x 2-inch pan. Layer cooked noodles and cheese. Add ground beef mixture. Top with additional cheese. Bake at 375 degrees for 35 to 40 minutes. Let stand for 5 to 10 minutes before serving.

# CRANBERRY PORK ROAST

1 lean, boneless pork roast (size can vary)
1 can jellied cranberry sauce
½ cup cranberry juice
½ cup sugar
1 teaspoon dry mustard
⅛ teaspoon ground cloves

Place roast in slow-cooker. Combine remaining ingredients and pour over roast. Cook on low for 6 to 8 hours. Thicken juice with cornstarch. Makes terrific gravy for mashed potatoes.

# BEEF TIPS WITH NOODLES

2 pounds lean stew meat, cut into bite-sized pieces
1 can cream of mushroom soup
1 package onion soup mix
1 cup lemon-lime soda
Cooked noodles or rice

Place meat in a 2-quart casserole dish. Pour soup and soup mix over meat. Add soda. Do not mix together or stir. Cover casserole and bake at 275 degrees for 4 hours. Do not open oven door during cooking. Let stand 30 minutes before serving. Serve over cooked noodles. May also serve over rice if preferred.

# MUSTARD GLAZED HAM

1 fully cooked ham, 8 to 10 pounds
1 small jar apple jelly
1 small jar pineapple preserves
1 (1 ounce) container dry mustard
2 tablespoons prepared horseradish
Salt and pepper

Bake ham at 325 degrees for 1 hour 45 minutes. Combine remaining ingredients and brush over ham. Return ham to oven for 35 to 45 minutes or until ham reaches 140 degrees.

# CREAMY BAKED CHICKEN BREASTS

4 boneless, skinless chicken breasts
4 slices Swiss cheese
1 can cream of chicken soup (thin with water to pour)
2 cups herb-seasoned stuffing mix
½ cup butter, melted (optional)

Preheat oven to 350 degrees. Place chicken in baking dish. Add cheese slice on top of each. Pour soup over all. Sprinkle with stuffing mix. Drizzle butter on top. Bake, uncovered, for 50 to 55 minutes.

# STUFFED HAM SLICE

2 cups soft breadcrumbs
½ cup raisins
½ cup chopped peanuts
2 tablespoons dark corn syrup
½ teaspoon dry mustard
¼ cup butter, melted
2 ½-inch thick ham slices
Whole cloves

Preheat oven to 300 degrees. Combine breadcrumbs, raisins, peanuts, corn syrup, mustard, and butter in large bowl. Mix well. Put 1 ham slice in baking dish. Spread with crumb mixture. Place second ham slice on top. Pierce fat of ham with cloves. Bake for 1 hour.

# CRESCENT ROLL CHICKEN

1 can cream of chicken soup
½ cup cheddar cheese, shredded (optional)
½ cup milk
1 tube refrigerated crescent rolls
3 boneless, skinless chicken breasts, cooked and cut into small pieces

Preheat oven to 350 degrees. Combine soup, cheese, and milk. Pour half into 13 x 9 x 2-inch pan. Separate rolls; place as much cut-up chicken in each roll as will fit; roll up, tucking in edges. Place in pan. Spoon other half of sauce over rolls. Sprinkle shredded cheese over all (optional). Bake for 25 to 30 minutes or until lightly browned.

Note: *If using 29-ounce can of chicken soup, use more cheese and 2 packages of crescent rolls.*

# TRADITIONAL CHRISTMAS TURKEY

1 (10 to 12 pound) whole turkey
6 tablespoons butter,
   sliced into pieces
3 cubes chicken bouillon
4 cups warm water

2 tablespoons dried parsley
2 tablespoons dried minced
   onion
2 tablespoons seasoned salt
2 tablespoons poultry seasoning

Preheat oven to 350 degrees. Rinse and wash turkey. Remove neck and discard giblets. Place turkey in roasting pan. Separate the skin over the breast and place slices of butter between the skin and breast meat. In medium bowl, dissolve bouillon in water. Stir in parsley and minced onion and pour mixture over top of turkey. Sprinkle turkey with seasoned salt and poultry seasoning. Cover with foil and bake 3½ to 4 hours, until internal temperature of turkey reaches 180 degrees. Remove foil during last 45 minutes to brown turkey.

# DELUXE ROAST BEEF

3 or more pounds roast beef
    (rump roast, bottom round, or eye of round)
1 to 2 onions, sliced
1 can cream of celery soup
1 can cream of mushroom soup
½ soup can of water

Line 13 x 9 x 2-inch baking dish with plenty of foil to cover and seal the meat. Preheat oven to 325 degrees. Trim excess fat from meat if desired. Place meat in center of foil-lined pan. Place onion slices on top and sides of meat. In medium-sized bowl, combine soups. Add water. Stir soup mixture well. Spoon over beef, moistening all visible meat. Seal in aluminum foil. Cook for about 45 minutes a pound.

# CREAMY BAKED CHICKEN

1 can condensed creamy chicken-mushroom soup, undiluted
4 chicken legs, skin removed
1½ teaspoons thyme
2 pounds sweet potatoes, peeled and cut into 2-inch chunks
3 cups frozen green peas

Preheat oven to 350 degrees. Spread soup over bottom of a Dutch oven. Add chicken legs. Coat thoroughly with soup. Sprinkle thyme over chicken. Add sweet potatoes. Bake for 50 minutes. Add peas; stir and cover. Bake 10 minutes longer or until chicken is no longer pink near the bone and the vegetables are tender.

# FAMILY DELIGHT HAM LOAF

2 or more pounds ground ham, according to taste
½ to 1 pound lean ground chuck
1 to 1½ cups bread crumbs
2 eggs, unbeaten
½ to 1 cup brown sugar
1 (15 to 16 ounce) can crushed pineapple, with juice
1 to 2 tablespoons mustard

Mix all ingredients together and press into glass or metal oblong baking dish. Bake at 350 degrees for 45 minutes to 1 hour. Cut into cubes. For a festive holiday treat, put a maraschino or candied cherry half on top of each cube.

# CHEESY BEEF TETRAZZINI

1½ pounds ground beef, browned and drained
1 (15 ounce) can tomato sauce
½ teaspoon salt
¼ teaspoon pepper
1 (8 ounce) package cream cheese, softened
1 cup small-curd cottage cheese
1 cup sour cream
¼ cup green pepper, chopped
1 small onion, chopped
¼ cup green onion, thinly sliced
1 (8 ounce) package thin spaghetti, cooked and drained
¼ cup grated Parmesan cheese

In a skillet, stir together cooked beef, tomato sauce, salt, and pepper. Bring to a boil. Reduce heat. Allow to simmer uncovered for 5 minutes. Meanwhile, beat cream cheese, cottage cheese, and sour cream until well blended. Add green pepper, onion, and spaghetti to cheese mixture. Transfer to a 1½-quart baking dish. Pour beef mixture over cheese mixture. Sprinkle with Parmesan cheese. Bake, uncovered, at 350 degrees for 30 to 35 minutes.

If desired, prepare casserole and refrigerate overnight. Bake right before serving.

# HOLIDAY HAM CASSEROLE

3 tablespoons butter
2 cups ham, cooked and cubed
1 (8½ ounce) can pineapple chunks, drained
1 (10½ ounce) can onion soup
3 tablespoons brown sugar
Salt and pepper to taste
1 (10½ ounce) can sweet potatoes, drained
½ cup chopped walnuts

In a large saucepan, heat butter and ham until lightly browned. Add pineapple chunks, onion soup, and 1 tablespoon brown sugar. Season with salt and pepper to taste. Bring to a boil, then remove from heat. Spoon into buttered casserole dish. Place sweet potato slices in an even layer over the ham and pineapple mixture. Combine walnuts and the remaining brown sugar. Spread this over the sweet potatoes. Bake for 30 minutes in a 400-degree oven.

# NEW YEAR'S CASSEROLE

2 pounds sausage
2 cups sauerkraut
1 large sweet onion, cut into rings
5 potatoes, sliced thin

Put in baking dish in layers, starting with sausage then sauerkraut, onion rings, and potatoes. Cover and bake at 375 degrees for 1½ hours or until potatoes are done. Uncover and brown for the last 15 minutes.

# SOUPS & SALADS

*I heard the bells on Christmas Day*
*Their old familiar carols play,*
*And wild and sweet the words repeat*
*Of peace on earth, good will to men.*

HENRY WADSWORTH LONGFELLOW

# BACON-CHEDDAR POTATO SOUP

½ pound bacon
1 cup onion
½ cup celery, chopped
½ cup flour
1 tablespoon seasoned salt
1 teaspoon white pepper

2 cups chicken stock
2 cups milk
4 cups diced potatoes, cooked
1 cup shredded sharp cheddar cheese
1 cup cubed Velveeta cheese
1 cup heavy cream

In a medium stock pot, fry bacon until crisp and remove from fat. Add onions and celery and cook. Add flour and seasonings. Add chicken stock, milk, and potatoes. Bring to a boil, stirring constantly. Reduce heat and add cheese, stirring until cheese is completely melted. Stir in heavy cream. Serve soup with crumbled bacon on top.

# BROCCOLI-CAULIFLOWER SALAD

1 head broccoli
1 head cauliflower
12 bacon slices,
    cooked and crumbled
1 small red onion, chopped

½ cup raisins
½ cup sunflower seed kernels
1 cup mayonnaise
½ cup sugar
2 tablespoons vinegar

Chop broccoli and cauliflower into bite-sized pieces and place in large mixing bowl. Add bacon, onion, raisins, and sunflower seeds. In another bowl, mix together mayonnaise, sugar, and vinegar. Pour mixture over salad and stir until well blended. Chill overnight.

# CREAM OF BROCCOLI SOUP

1 (10 ounce) package frozen chopped broccoli
Onion or onion powder to taste
1 can chicken broth
1 can condensed cream of celery soup
1 can condensed cream of mushroom soup
1 to 1½ cups cheddar cheese, shredded

Cook broccoli and onion in chicken broth. Combine soups and stir into broccoli mixture. Bring to a gentle boil, stirring constantly. Add cheese, stirring until melted. Serve hot.
Yield: 6 servings

# CREAMY TOMATO BACON SOUP MIX

2 tablespoons Italian seasoning

1 teaspoon salt

¼ teaspoon pepper

3 tablespoons flour

⅓ cup plus 3 tablespoons
    powdered milk

¼ cup original coffee creamer

⅛ cup dried onion flakes

½ cup real bacon bits

1 bay leaf

¾ cup dried tomatoes

Combine Italian seasoning, salt, pepper, and flour; then add powdered milk, creamer, and onion flakes. In a 1-pint jar, layer milk mixture then bacon bits. Slip bay leaf in the front of the jar, making sure bacon bits hold half of it in place. Complete layering with dried tomatoes. Seal. Attach a recipe card with the following instructions:

# CREAMY TOMATO BACON SOUP

2 cups water

Creamy Tomato Bacon Soup Mix

1 (28 ounce) can diced tomatoes

Bring 2 cups of water to a boil in a saucepan. Briskly stir in Creamy Tomato Bacon Soup Mix. After mixture is smooth, add canned tomatoes, cooking until mixture boils, stirring constantly. Makes approximately 6 servings.

GIFT IDEA: *Place Creamy Tomato Bacon Soup Mix in a basket with crackers and cheese.*

# Slow-Cooker Chili

1 pound ground beef
1 medium yellow onion, diced
1 (15¼ ounce) can chili beans
1 packet chili seasoning mix
1 (28 ounce) can Italian-style diced tomatoes

Brown and drain ground beef and onion. Add all ingredients to a slow-cooker. Cook on low for 2 to 4 hours.

# CREAM OF PUMPKIN SOUP

1 cup onion, chopped

2 tablespoons butter, melted

2 (14.5 ounce) cans
   chicken broth

1 (15 ounce) can pumpkin

1 teaspoon salt

¼ teaspoon cinnamon

⅛ teaspoon ginger

⅛ teaspoon pepper

1 cup half-and-half

In a medium saucepan, sauté onion in butter until tender. Slowly add 1 can chicken broth; stir well. Bring to a boil; cover, reduce heat, and simmer 15 minutes. Transfer broth mixture into blender or food processor. Process until smooth. Return processed mixture to saucepan. Stir in remaining can of broth, pumpkin, and spices. Bring to a boil; cover, reduce heat, and simmer 10 minutes, stirring occasionally. Stir in half-and-half and heat through. Do not boil. Garnish as desired.

# Corn Chowder

½ pound bacon
½ cup onion, chopped
½ cup celery, chopped
2 tablespoons flour
4 cups milk

⅛ teaspoon black pepper
2 cans cream-style corn
Fresh parsley, chopped
Paprika

In a saucepan, fry bacon until crisp. Remove bacon from pan, crumble, and set aside. Drain fat, reserving 3 tablespoons in saucepan. Cook onion and celery in bacon drippings until tender; remove from heat. Stir in flour. Cook over medium heat, stirring constantly, until mixture is bubbly; remove from heat. Stir in milk. Heat to boiling, stirring constantly. Boil and stir for 1 minute. Reduce heat. Stir in pepper and corn. Cook until soup is heated through. Remove from heat and ladle into soup bowls.

# ITALIAN RICE SOUP MIX

1½ cups uncooked long grain brown rice
⅓ cup chicken bouillon granules
3 teaspoons dried parsley flakes
3 teaspoons Italian seasoning
¾ teaspoon freshly ground pepper

In a medium bowl, combine all ingredients. Spoon soup mix into a 1-pint glass jar. Attach a recipe card with the following instructions:

# ITALIAN RICE SOUP

3 cups water
1 tablespoon butter
⅔ cup Italian Rice Soup Mix

In a medium saucepan, bring water, butter, and Italian Rice Soup Mix to a boil. Reduce heat; cover and simmer for 30 to 35 minutes or until rice is tender.

# BROCCOLI CHEESE SOUP

½ cup onions, chopped
¼ cup butter or margarine
5 cups water
3 tablespoons chicken base
1 (28 ounce) package fine noodles
2 (12 ounce) packages frozen broccoli
5 cups milk
2 pounds cubed Velveeta cheese

In a large pot, sauté onions in melted butter. Add water, chicken base, and noodles. Cook until noodles are tender. Add broccoli and cook for 5 minutes. Add milk and Velveeta cheese. Cook about 1 hour or until cheese is melted.

# BAKED POTATO SOUP

⅔ cup butter
½ cup onion, diced
⅔ cup flour
6 cups milk
4 large baking potatoes,
    baked

Salt and pepper, to taste
½ cup cheddar cheese, shredded
1 (8 ounce) carton sour cream
Additional sour cream, chopped
    green onions, cooked and
    crumbled bacon for topping

In a large saucepan, melt butter. Add onions and sauté until clear. Add flour a little at a time and whisk into a paste. Add milk 1 cup at a time, whisking constantly; allow to thicken in between each addition. Cut potatoes into bite-sized pieces. When soup is desired thickness, slowly stir in potato pieces. Add salt and pepper to taste. Just before serving, mix in cheese and sour cream. Ladle into bowls and garnish with toppings.

# Frozen Cranberry Salad

2 (3 ounce) packages cream cheese, softened
2 tablespoons mayonnaise or salad dressing
2 cups whipped topping
2 tablespoons sugar
Pinch salt
1 (8 ounce) can crushed pineapple, drained
½ cup pecans or walnuts, chopped
2 cups flaked coconut (optional)
1 (14 ounce) can cranberry sauce, jelled

In a medium bowl, blend cream cheese and salad dressing. Fold in whipped topping; set aside. In a large mixing bowl, combine sugar, salt, pineapple, nuts, coconut, and cranberry sauce. Gently combine with cream cheese mixture. Spread into 13 x 9 x 2-inch pan. Cover and freeze. Thaw 10 to 15 minutes before serving. Cut into squares.

# WALDORF SALAD

White grapes
2 cups apples, diced
1 cup celery, diced
½ cup chopped nuts

¼ cup mayonnaise
1 tablespoon sugar
1 teaspoon lemon juice
½ cup whipped topping

Mix grapes, apples, celery, and nuts. In a separate bowl, mix mayonnaise, sugar, and lemon juice. Add to fruit mixture. Fold in whipped topping.

# CHERRY CRANBERRY JELL-O SALAD

1 cup water (or syrup drained from pineapple)
2 (3 ounce) packages cherry gelatin
1 cup lemon-lime soda, chilled
1 (1 pound) can whole cranberry sauce
1 (9 ounce) can crushed pineapple, drained
½ cup celery, chopped
¼ cup nuts, chopped

In a saucepan, heat water or syrup to boiling. Add to gelatin, stirring until dissolved. Add soda. Chill until syrupy. Fold in cranberry sauce, then add pineapple, celery, and nuts. Pour into a 5-cup mold and chill until firm.

# FRESH BROCCOLI SALAD

1 package fresh broccoli

3 stalks celery (or 1 large Vidalia onion)

1 cup raisins

½ cup bacon bits (or 6 slices cooked, crumbled bacon)

1 tablespoon vinegar

1 teaspoon sugar

3 tablespoons mayonnaise

Chop florets of broccoli and celery (or onion). Add other ingredients. Mix with mayonnaise. Chill for 1 hour or longer.

# CINNAMON APPLESAUCE SALAD

½ cup red hot candies
2 cups boiling water
2 (3 ounce) packages cherry or strawberry gelatin
2 cups unsweetened applesauce

Dissolve candies in boiling water. Stir in gelatin and dissolve. Stir in applesauce. Pour into baking pan or gelatin mold and chill until firm.

# FRESH CRANBERRY SALAD

2 cups water
¾ cup sugar
3 cups (12 ounces) fresh cranberries
1 (6 ounce) package orange-flavored gelatin
1 (8.25 ounce) can crushed pineapple
½ cup celery or walnuts, chopped
Salad greens

Place water and sugar in 2-quart saucepan and bring to a boil; boil for 1 minute. Add cranberries and return to a boil for 5 minutes. Add gelatin and stir until dissolved. Stir in pineapple (including liquid) and celery or walnuts. Pour into 6-cup mold and chill at least 6 hours, until firm. Unmold onto salad greens. Garnish with pineapple chunks and sour cream if desired.

# Frozen Fruit Salad

2 ripe bananas
1 (16 ounce) can pineapple juice
2 tablespoons lemon juice
1 cup orange juice
½ cup mayonnaise or salad dressing
1 (10 ounce) can mandarin oranges, undrained
¼ cup sugar
Iceberg lettuce

In blender combine bananas, pineapple juice, and lemon juice. Blend 1 minute on low speed until smooth. Add orange juice, mayonnaise or salad dressing, oranges, and sugar; whirl ½ minute on low. Freeze 4 hours in six 6-ounce molds or one 9 x 9 x 2-inch pan. When ready to serve, cut and place on a lettuce leaf. Use as a dessert or salad.

# Raspberry Mandarin Orange Jell-O Mold

2 large packages raspberry gelatin
2 cups boiling water
1 can applesauce
2 (10 ounce) boxes frozen raspberries with syrup, thawed
2 small cans mandarin oranges with juice

Dissolve gelatin in boiling water. Add applesauce; stir thoroughly. Stir in fruits. Pour into Jell-O mold or Bundt pan. Chill until set.

# CHERRY DELIGHT

1 can cherry pie filling
1 can crushed pineapple, drained
1 (14 ounce) can sweetened condensed milk
1 (8 ounce) carton whipped topping, thawed
1 cup pecans, coarsely chopped

Blend first 3 ingredients. Fold in whipped topping and pecans. Chill overnight until firm. This can also be frozen.

# HOLIDAY SHERBET SALAD

1 (6 ounce) package strawberry gelatin
2 cups boiling water
1 pint raspberry sherbet
1 (20 ounce) can crushed pineapple, drained
1 cup miniature marshmallows
1 (8 ounce) carton whipped topping

Dissolve gelatin completely in boiling water. Stir in sherbet. Chill until partially set, then mix in pineapple and marshmallows. Fold in whipped topping. Chill until firm.

# Veggies & Sides

---

*It was always said of him, that he knew how to keep Christmas well, if any man alive possessed the knowledge. May that be truly said of us, and all of us! And so, as Tiny Tim observed, "God bless us, every one!"*

Charles Dickens

# CLASSIC GREEN BEAN BAKE

1 (10¾ ounce) can cream of mushroom soup
½ cup milk
1 teaspoon soy sauce
Dash pepper
4 cups cut green beans, cooked
1 (2.8 ounce) can French-fried onions

Preheat oven to 350 degrees. Combine soup, milk, soy sauce, and pepper in a 1½-quart casserole dish. Stir in beans and half of the onions. Bake until hot (about 25 minutes). Stir the mixture and top with the remaining onions. Bake 5 minutes longer.

# SCALLOPED CORN

2 pints frozen corn, thawed
2 eggs
1 tablespoon butter or margarine,
   melted

2 tablespoons flour
2 tablespoons sugar
½ teaspoon salt
Dash pepper

Mix all ingredients in a casserole dish. Bake at 325 degrees for 1 hour.

# BAKED POTATO CASSEROLE

4 large baking potatoes, baked and cubed
1 pound bacon, fried and crumbled
1 (8 ounce) carton sour cream
4 ounces cream cheese, softened
1 cup cheddar cheese, shredded
4 green onions, chopped
Salt and pepper to taste

Preheat oven to 350 degrees. Blend all ingredients well. Bake until heated through and cheese is melted, approximately 30 minutes.

# CARROT SOUFFLÉ

2 pounds cooked carrots

2 cups sugar

6 eggs

1 cup butter or margarine

6 tablespoons flour

2 teaspoons baking powder

2 teaspoons vanilla

Preheat oven to 350 degrees. Blend or mash carrots; gradually add other ingredients, adding baking powder and vanilla last. Beat until smooth. Place in casserole. Bake for 30 to 45 minutes, until firm.

# CHEESY VEGGIE CASSEROLE

2 bags frozen broccoli/cauliflower/carrot mixture, thawed
1 pound processed cheese, cubed
1 roll butter-flavor crackers, crushed
½ cup butter, melted

Preheat oven to 350 degrees. Pour vegetables into greased baking dish. Add cheese and distribute evenly. Sprinkle crushed crackers over vegetables and cheese and drizzle with melted butter. Bake for 35 to 40 minutes or until cheese is melted and bubbly.

# CORN CASSEROLE

1 can sweet whole kernel corn, drained
2 eggs, lightly beaten
1 small box corn muffin mix
½ cup butter, melted
1 (8 ounce) container sour cream

Preheat oven to 350 degrees. Combine all ingredients. Place in greased 9 x 9-inch baking pan. Bake for 45 to 50 minutes or until golden brown.

# Broccoli and Rice

2 (10 ounce) packages frozen chopped broccoli
2 cups cooked rice
1 teaspoon celery salt
3 cups cubed Velveeta cheese

Cook broccoli according to package directions. Drain completely. Add rice and celery salt. Stir in Velveeta until melted and all ingredients are completely mixed. Serve warm.

# CREAMED CARROT BAKE

2 pounds carrots, peeled and sliced
2 (3 ounce) packages cream cheese, softened
¼ cup butter
2 teaspoons sugar
1 package stuffing mix

Preheat oven to 350 degrees. Cook carrots in salted water until tender. Drain well. Combine cream cheese, butter, and sugar. Carefully stir carrots into cream cheese mixture. Pour into 1½-quart buttered casserole dish. Sprinkle with dry stuffing mix. Bake for 20 minutes or until heated through.

# GOLDEN SQUASH CASSEROLE

6 cups cubed, pared Hubbard squash
1 cup sour cream
2 tablespoons butter or margarine
1 medium onion, finely chopped
1 teaspoon salt
¼ teaspoon black pepper

Place 1 inch of salted water in pan and bring to a boil. Add squash, cover, and return to a boil. Cook for 15 to 20 minutes or until tender; drain. After mashing squash, stir in remaining ingredients. Pour into ungreased 1-quart casserole. Bake, uncovered, at 325 degrees for 35 to 45 minutes or until hot.

NOTE: *Two packages (12 ounces each) frozen cooked squash, thawed, can be substituted for the fresh squash.*

# CAULIFLOWER WITH CHEESE SAUCE

2 tablespoons butter
2 tablespoons flour
¼ teaspoon salt
⅛ teaspoon pepper

1 cup milk
½ cup cheddar cheese, cubed
2 (10 ounce) packages
    frozen cauliflower

In a heavy saucepan, melt butter over low heat. Blend in flour and seasonings. Cook over low heat, stirring until mixture is smooth and bubbly. Remove from heat. Stir in milk. Bring to boil, stirring constantly. Boil 1 minute. Add cheese and stir until melted and well blended. Set aside. Cook cauliflower according to package directions. Drain. Pour cheese sauce over cauliflower.

# GREEN BEANS ALMONDINE

4 slices bacon
½ cup sugar
½ cup vinegar
1 medium onion, sliced thin

2 (15 ounce) cans green beans, drained
½ cup slivered almonds

In a skillet, fry bacon until crisp. Set aside. Add sugar and vinegar to bacon drippings. Separate the onion into rings and place in skillet, then add beans and almonds. Cover and simmer for 25 minutes. Place in serving dish and sprinkle with crumbled bacon.

# HASH BROWN POTATO CASSEROLE

1 (2 pound) bag frozen hash browns
½ cup butter or margarine, melted
½ to 1 teaspoon salt
½ teaspoon black pepper
1 can cream of chicken soup (regular or reduced fat/sodium)
1 pint sour cream (regular or low-fat)
¼ cup onion, chopped
8 to 10 ounces cheddar cheese, shredded
2 cups ham, cooked and diced (optional)
1 cup cornflakes
3 tablespoons butter, melted

Mix all ingredients except cornflakes and melted butter. Pour in large baking dish. Sprinkle top with cornflakes and butter. Bake at 350 degrees for 1½ hours.

VARIATION: *Add 1 can cream of potato soup (regular or reduced fat/ low-sodium) in place of the cream of chicken soup.*

# MIXED VEGETABLES WITH SAUCE

¾ cup mayonnaise
1 small onion, diced
½ tablespoon Worcestershire sauce
2 hard-boiled eggs, diced
1 tablespoon oil
½ tablespoon prepared mustard
1 small can water chestnuts, sliced
1 (20 ounce) bag frozen mixed vegetables

Mix all ingredients except mixed vegetables. Set aside. Cook frozen vegetables about 15 minutes or until barely done. Drain. Add sauce. Serve immediately or refrigerate and use as a salad.

# PARTY POTATOES

10 to 12 medium potatoes, cooked and mashed
1 (8 ounce) package cream cheese
1 cup sour cream
2 tablespoons chopped chives
1 cup shredded cheddar cheese
Salt and pepper to taste
2 tablespoons butter

Beat together first 7 ingredients. Place in greased 13 x 9 x 2-inch baking dish. Cover and refrigerate until 1 hour before serving time. Preheat oven to 350 degrees. Dot potatoes with butter. Bake for 1 hour or until potatoes are thoroughly heated.

# LAYERED SALAD

1 head lettuce, shredded

2 cucumbers, diced

2 tomatoes, diced

1 medium onion, diced

6 radishes, thinly sliced

1 medium bell pepper, diced

1 pound bacon, cooked and crumbled

Salt and black pepper to taste

1 (3 ounce) can English peas, drained

1 (3 ounce) can sweet whole kernel corn, drained

2 cups mayonnaise

1 pound cheddar cheese, shredded

Arrange salad ingredients in large casserole or oblong pan, one at a time, layering as you go. Spread mayonnaise over salad ingredients and sprinkle cheddar cheese on top. Serve using an egg turner.

# BACON CHEESE POTATOES

2½ to 3 pounds potatoes
½ cup onion, finely chopped
1 pound American cheese, cubed
1 cup mayonnaise
½ pound sliced bacon, cooked and crumbled
¾ cup ripe olives, sliced

Cook potatoes until tender. Cut into cubes. Put potatoes in a bowl and add onions, cheese, and mayonnaise. Transfer mixture to a 13 x 9 x 2-inch baking dish. Sprinkle bacon and olives over mixture. Bake at 350 degrees for 35 minutes.

# Mushroom Pecan Rice

1 cup brown rice, uncooked

½ teaspoon nutmeg

1 (10¾ ounce) can cream of mushroom soup, undiluted

1 (4 ounce) can mushroom stems and pieces, drained

½ cup pecans, coarsely chopped

2 tablespoons butter, melted

Cook rice according to package directions. Combine rice with nutmeg, mushroom soup, and mushroom pieces. Pour mixture into a greased 2-quart baking dish; set aside. Sauté pecans in butter until they are lightly toasted. Sprinkle over rice mixture. Bake at 350 degrees for 20 minutes.

# PECAN SWEET POTATOES

6 medium sweet potatoes, baked, cooled, and peeled
½ cup brown sugar
½ cup pecans, chopped
1 tablespoon orange peel
1 cup orange juice
1½ tablespoons butter, cut up
½ teaspoon salt

Lightly spray 13 x 9 x 2-inch baking pan with nonstick cooking spray. Slice potatoes in ¼-inch slices, layer in pan, and set aside. In a small bowl, combine brown sugar, pecans, and orange peel. Pour mixture over sweet potatoes. Pour orange juice over all. Dot with butter. Season with salt to taste. Cover and refrigerate until ready to use. Bake at 350 degrees for 45 minutes; uncover and cook 15 to 20 minutes longer.

# ROASTED POTATO BITES

12 to 15 small red potatoes
1 cup cheddar cheese, shredded
½ cup real or light mayonnaise
½ cup green onion, minced
½ pound bacon, cooked and crumbled
2 tablespoons fresh basil, chopped

Bake potatoes until tender. Allow to cool enough to handle. Cut cross-
wise in half. Cut a thin slice from bottom so they stand upright. Scoop
out potatoes, leaving ¼-inch rim in shell. Combine scooped potatoes
with rest of ingredients. Spoon into potato shells. Bake at 375 degrees
for 3 to 5 minutes or until brown. Serve hot.

# Slow-Cooker Ranch Potatoes

1 (24 ounce) bag frozen hash browns, partially thawed
1 (8 ounce) package cream cheese, softened
1 (1 ounce) envelope dry ranch dressing mix
1 can cream of potato soup

In a large mixing bowl, mix ingredients together well. Pour into slow-cooker and cook on low 6 to 8 hours or until potatoes test done and casserole is heated throughout.

# MARY'S CORN PUDDING

1 pint fresh corn, with pulp
   scraped from cob
2 egg yolks
1½ tablespoons flour
1 cup whole milk

1 tablespoon sugar
1 tablespoon melted butter
½ teaspoon salt
Dash black pepper
2 egg whites, beaten to stiff peaks

Preheat oven to 350 degrees. In a large bowl, combine corn, egg yolks, flour, milk, sugar, butter, salt, and pepper. Mix well. Fold in egg whites. Turn into a buttered baking dish, and bake for 30 to 35 minutes or until set.

# OLD-FASHIONED BREAD STUFFING

½ cup butter
1 cup chopped sweet onion
½ cup chopped celery,
   with leaves
8 cups bread cubes
2 tablespoons hot chicken
   or turkey broth

1 teaspoon salt
¼ teaspoon pepper
1 teaspoon sage
½ teaspoon thyme
½ teaspoon marjoram

Melt butter in frying pan. Add onion and celery, and cook until soft but not browned. Combine butter mixture with bread cubes, broth, and seasonings. For a soft, moist dressing, use fresh or slightly stale bread. For a lighter, fluffier dressing, use dried, stale bread. Makes enough to stuff an 8- to 10-pound turkey.

# STUFFED WINTER SQUASH

3 small acorn or butternut squash
1 large sweet onion, diced
1 tablespoon olive oil
1 cup finely diced celery
1 cup fresh spinach, coarsely chopped
1 cup whole wheat bread crumbs
¼ teaspoon salt
¼ cup finely ground almonds
2 tablespoons butter

Clean squash and cut each in half. Bake at 350 degrees for 35 minutes or until tender. Sauté onions in oil until soft. Add diced celery. Cover and simmer on medium heat until tender. Add spinach; stir to wilt. Combine bread crumbs with salt and ground nuts. Stuff squash halves with spinach mixture, and sprinkle the crumb mixture on top. Dot with butter. Return to oven for 10 to 15 minutes.

# INDEX

## BREADS

## Candies

## Cookies

## Main Dishes

## Soups & Salads

# INDEX